"Every member of Congress, and every judge, should read this book. Ruth Colker cuts through the rhetoric of laissez-faire economics that dominates legislative and judicial decision-making and exposes its theoretical fallacies and practical harms. Why do we consider the worker, the family, and the state to be three separate, independent units? Colker challenges us to consider an America in which the state plays a more active role in ensuring the health and well-being of its families and workers. Instead of the regressive and punitive policies of the recent Congress, in areas ranging from welfare to disability payments to immigration, Colker offers us a vision of a country that combines capitalism and nurturance. Her book comes at a critical juncture in our national debate on social welfare and policy. Let us hope its lessons are absorbed by our leaders."

—Chai R. Feldblum

Director, Federal ̲  ̲ on Clinic

̲  w Center

## Other Books by Ruth Colker

*Hybrid: Bisexual, Multiracials, and Other Misfits under American Law*
(1996)

*Pregnant Men: Practice, Theory and the Law*
(1994)

*Abortion & Dialogue: Pro-Choice, Pro-Life and American Law*
(1992)

# AMERICAN LAW IN THE AGE OF HYPERCAPITALISM

The Worker, the Family, and the State

Ruth Colker

NEW YORK UNIVERSITY PRESS
New York and London

**NEW YORK UNIVERSITY PRESS**
New York and London

Library of Congress Cataloging-in-Publication Data
Colker, Ruth.
American law in the age of hypercapitalism : the worker, the
family, and the state / Ruth Colker.
p.    cm. — (Critical America)
Includes index.
ISBN 0-8147-1562-1 (cloth : alk. paper).
ISBN 0-8147-1563-X (pbk. : alk. paper)
1. Labor laws and legislation—United States. 2. Discrimination
in employment—Law and legislation—United States. 3. Critical
legal studies—United States. 4. Capitalism—United States. 5. Law
and economics. 6. Sociological jurisprudence. I. Title. II. Series.
KF3455.Z9C65    1998
344.7301—dc21              94–33959
                                CIP

New York University Press books are printed on acid-free paper,
and their binding materials are chosen for strength and durability.

Manufactured in the United States of America
10  9  8  7  6  5  4  3  2  1

for Sammy, Julia, and Sasha,
and the other babies of 1997
May they thrive in a society that
genuinely respects its children

# CONTENTS

# PREFACE

The idea for this book began to develop in the fall of 1988 when I visited the University of Toronto Faculty of Law. Like most Americans, I knew very little about Canadian law and society. I did not expect Canada's legal regime to differ much from ours, and I did expect its legal system to reflect a respect for our two hundred years of constitutional jurisprudence. What I learned about Canadian constitutional law was that its protection of individual rights differed markedly from the American model. For example, while the United States was involved in a bitter fight over affirmative action, Canada's Charter of Rights protected it. Whereas the United States was considering whether to adopt any federal family leave policy at all (and, of course, only unpaid leave), the government of Ontario was expanding its already generous family leave legislation to encompass the possibility of nearly one year of paid leave.

The possibility of a different balance among the state, the employer, and the family became even more apparent when I was asked to give the keynote address at a disability rights conference sponsored by Griffiths University in Brisbane, Australia, in 1996. Visiting Australia gave me an opportunity to learn more about how other common law countries had developed laws regarding disability discrimination. My research on the laws of Australia, Canada, and the recently passed law of Great Britain revealed great divergence among these countries. Although the United States was the first of these countries to pass a comprehensive statute to protect against disability discrimination, as interpreted by the courts its current protections are often the narrowest of these countries.

I also heard a different style of rhetoric in Australia, compared with the United States, in regard to the state's obligation to persons with disabilities. Whereas the United States' rhetoric is often based on the presumptions of a laissez-faire economy, Australia's rhetoric usually presumes that the state should have an active role in the lives of all its citizens.

This opportunity to study the legal systems of Canada and Australia gave me a new perspective on the presumptions of the American legal system. It has become commonplace in American law schools to presume that "law and economics" will dominate legal decisions with their consideration of utility and efficiency. Increasingly, we have not asked our students to consider the human values that underlie our choices within the law. This presumption also extends to the political arena, in which politicians compete over how much they can cut back on aid to poor mothers, without considering the impact on our next generation of children. The debate about social welfare in Canada and Australia seems more embedded in the human values of love and compassion toward our present and next generation.

The subtitle of this book—*The Worker, the Family, and the State*—reflects the tripartite division that we usually see in the United States when we discuss the worker and the family. Although our usual presumption is that these categories are three separate units, it is time that we began to see that parenting *is* work and that the state *should* play a crucial role in easing the family responsibilities of parents, regardless of how much money they earn outside their home. Other countries have a more integrated notion of the worker, the family, and the state, but without moving toward a socialist economic system.

These comparative observations led me to conclude, reluctantly, that the United States has moved toward what in this book I term *hypercapitalism*—a capitalism that is overly enamored with laissez-faire economics and insufficiently concerned with our health and well-being. Fortunately, the tide may be turning. Even financier George Soros recently criticized America's devotion to hypercapitalism. Accordingly, I hope that this book arrives at a good moment in our national debate about the relationship between the citizen and the state and that I can help put back the needs of people into the American model of capitalism.

# ACKNOWLEDGMENTS

The problem with writing acknowledgements is that one is bound to forget to thank lots of people who were of tremendous assistance. Casual conversations with colleagues at conferences, brief conversations in the halls of the law school, insightful comments from seminar students, and help in the library from whoever was at the reference desk at the moment helped make this book possible, yet my memories are not sufficiently specific to offer appropriate thanks. So, first, thanks to all the people who provide the background support in my life that I probably take too easily for granted.

As for those people whom I especially want to name, let me start with my editor at New York University Press, Niko Pfund. Even after becoming director of the press, Niko stayed faithful to my project. He's probably read some chapters more often than I have. He sent me books and articles as well as captivating ideas. I hope I have been as responsive to his many suggestions as he has been responsive to my never-ending queries.

Theresa ("Tish") Zimmerman, my research assistant at the University of Pittsburgh School of Law, also offered enormous assistance. I wrote the first draft of this book while pregnant and had little inclination to walk all over the Pitt campus to find books and research material. Tish thus often served as my legs, spending many hours in the Economics Library finding material for me. After I gave birth, her diligence continued as she brought material to my home while I was on maternity leave from the office.

My colleagues Jules Lobel (law) and Lisa Brush (sociology) also deserve a special note of thanks. On our runs together, Jules helped me conceptualize the basic idea behind this book through his critique of capitalism. Lisa introduced me to writers in sociology who also use a sophisticated economic analysis. Both of them listened to my hypotheses and insights with patience and inquisitiveness. I hope this final product doesn't disappoint them.

And then there are the countless people who heard me deliver drafts of various chapters at conferences and were generous with their responses. Chapter 2 received some assistance from my Canadian colleagues at the University of Alberta, who invited me to write that chapter for a symposium on U.S. and Canadian constitutional law. My Australian colleagues, whom I met at a symposium on disability rights at Griffith University in Queensland, helped with the argument developed in chapter 3. Brian Doyle, a professor in Great Britain, also offered valuable assistance with that chapter. A workshop sponsored by the University of Illinois Law School gave me invaluable assistance for both the first and third chapters and particularly helped me develop my definition of capitalism. The participants at a symposium sponsored by the *Yale Journal of Law and Feminism* in the fall of 1996 was critical to the development of the ideas in chapters 4 and 6. The participants at a symposium sponsored by the *Hastings Law Journal* in the winter of 1997 also helped me formulate the thesis of chapter 5. Finally, Daniel Posin (Tulane University) offered me a wonderfully constructive "blind" review at the final stages of the project. Thus, with help from colleagues in Canada, Great Britain, and Australia, as well as the United States, I feel fortunate to have been able to write this book in a truly multinational context.

The Document Technology Center at the University of Pittsburgh School of Law made a typically fine contribution to this project. The high quality of its work coupled with a miraculous turnaround time made writing pleasurable instead of drudgery. The financial support of the School of Law for this project is also greatly appreciated. Dean Peter Shane allowed me to use extra research assistance at a time of fiscal austerity and was flexible with my maternity leave so that I could finish this project. I was fortunate to finish this project with the support of my new home—the Ohio State University College of Law. Dean Gregory Williams agreed to support this project even before I had moved my family to Columbus, Ohio, and therefore made it possible for me to finish this project in Pittsburgh even while organizing a relocation to Columbus.

And as always, I would like to thank my family for their support while I wrote this book. My husband, Edward Eybel, helped take care of the children and the household chores while I pounded away on the keyboard; my five-year-old, Cara Colker-Eybel, learned to respect my office space so that she could play computer games without ruining my work, and my infant, Samuel Colker-Eybel, cooperated by sitting quietly in his chair while I typed away. I feel fortunate to have been able to combine family, work, pregnancy, and childbirth while writing this book. I hope that we can develop policies that give more people the opportunities that I have had, to spend time with their children while experiencing a fulfilling career.

# 1

## THE TATTERED SAFETY NET

Isabelle Dumont, a legal immigrant to the United States from Haiti, works for the Bayer family. In return for taking care of their children while they are at work each day (from at least 8 A.M. until 6 P.M.), she is paid $250 per week. When the family goes on vacation, she has her own (unpaid) vacation. Because she is not a U.S. citizen, Isabelle is not eligible for Medicaid, and she cannot afford private health insurance on her modest wages. Isabelle brings her own daughter, Medina, to work with her each day and finds it exhausting to juggle the child care responsibilities of another family's children along with those of her own. Isabelle is worried about retiring someday because the Bayers do not contribute to Social Security on her behalf. When she asks about this, Mrs. Bayer tells her it is in her best interest that they do not, because if *they did, Isabelle would also be responsible for Social Security taxes.*

*When Isabelle heard that the federal minimum wage was being raised, she asked Mr. Bayer if she was entitled to a pay increase. Mr. Bayer smiled and said, "You're not covered by federal wage and hour laws because you are a domestic worker." Because Isabelle's immigration status is dependent on her being employed with the Bayers, she has to look the other way when Mr. Bayer makes lewd comments or touches her in ways that she finds unwelcome.*

*Isabelle lives on the margins of American society. If she becomes pregnant again, she can expect no assistance from the state. Even if she becomes a U.S. citizen, she would have to work for an employer who employed more than fifty people in order to qualify for twelve weeks of unpaid leave (which she could never afford) after giving birth. Even her poor, native Haiti has better maternity benefits than the rich United States does. And her quality of life would fall even lower if she developed any of the disabilities that seem to run in her family—diabetes and hypertension in particular—because of the few health insurance benefits and work opportunities available to her.*

*Even though Isabelle keeps hearing that America has great civil rights laws, they do not apply to her because she is part of the underpaid contingent workforce. She is hoping that her daughter will do well enough in school to win a college scholarship someday, but she has been warned that the special scholarship programs for racial minorities have been eliminated in her state following a recent Supreme Court decision. It does not seem fair to her that the Bayers are confident that their children will attend Harvard someday, since both parents are alumni of that institution. When Mr. Bayer sends in his contri-*

bution to the school each year, he chuckles that it is really his children's insurance policy.

Isabelle has considered trying to juggle school with a part-time job in order to become a licensed practical nurse. It is unlikely, however, that she would find the conditions in that profession any better than those in her current situation. Not only do licensed practical nurses have to perform more and more menial jobs because of the continual layoffs of nurses, but they also are not allowed to unionize because at their $7 per hour wage, they are considered to be "supervisors" exempt from the labor law's protection. Ironically, highly paid professional employees like airline pilots are allowed to join a union. In the United States, it is hard to understand who is worker and who is management.

Isabelle has heard that the best nanny jobs these days involve working for people with political aspirations. Such employers actually seem to fear that they may someday be criticized for shirking their responsibilities to pay Social Security taxes. But these people also are not hiring recent immigrants. Indeed, some of them are actually hiring unemployed white elementary schoolteachers to cradle their infants. Isabelle has seen these high-priced nannies at the park—they have no idea how to calm a screaming infant or discipline a bratty child. Their academic degree, she realizes, makes them qualified in a way that she cannot match, despite her decades of child care experience. She is determined that her own daughter will have the credentials that matter in this capitalist society so that she, too, can hire someone to take care of her children. America is the land of opportunity, she remembers. Whose opportunities, she wonders. . . .

Isabelle's friends who emigrated to Canada report a different story. They have health insurance, and those who live in Quebec *receive some state support if they have children. In Canada, immigrants can work in child care centers where they actually earn a living wage with several paid weeks of vacation each year. (Isabelle has inquired about working at the local child care center, but the conditions and benefits are no better than at the Bayer residence.) From Isabelle's perspective in Haiti, North America looked like a uniform monolith. She is now beginning to wish she had heeded people's warnings that despite its thriving economy, America's version of capitalism is actually impoverished.*

Isabelle's story goes virtually unheard in the United States. When Zoe Baird and Kimba Wood were unable to be confirmed as U.S. attorney general because they had employed noncitizen nannies, the political response was to expand the Social Security exemption for these wealthy employers rather than to try to improve the nannies' working conditions. Little thought was given to the fact that the United States' treatment of domestic workers harms the workers themselves as well as the country's next generation of children. Working parents scramble everyday to find safe and nurturing environments for their children, with almost no federal subsidy of child care, whereas wealthy parents receive increasing subsidies for their use of low-paid immigrant labor in their homes.

This book tells Isabelle's side of the story. Chapter 2 questions why affirmative action for privileged white people in the form of alumni preferences go unnoticed while affirmative action for racial minorities is criticized and said to contribute to the "stigmatization" of racial minorities. Why is no stigma attached to the privileges extended to the ultrarich? In chapter 3, I compare judicial interpretations of the Americans with Disabilities

Act with interpretations of similar statutes in Canada, Australia, and Great Britain. Although the United States was historically the leader in enacting protection against disability discrimination in employment, the United States is the only one of these countries that sometimes excludes from coverage people with insulin-dependent diabetes or hypertension. Why do U.S. courts render such narrow interpretations of disability discrimination law? In chapter 4, I discuss pregnancy-related issues, in which the United States consistently fails to provide meaningful protection to pregnant women, fetuses, or newborn children, in comparison with Canada and western Europe. Why does the United States not show more concern for the well-being of the next generation? Chapter 5 connects the homophobia underlying American law and the country's militaristic and moralistic style of capitalism. Why do the principles of laissez-faire capitalism disappear when issues involving gay men and lesbians arise under the law? In chapter 6, Isabelle's plight is connected to that of all unprotected workers in the United States—the contingent workforce consisting of nearly one-third of all American workers and especially women, the poor, racial minorities, and recent immigrants. Why does the United States consistently exclude the most underprivileged workers from meaningful workplace protection? The last chapter considers the story of Isabelle's daughter, Medina. She will be sorely disappointed if she expects the principles of laissez-faire capitalism to apply to her dreams and aspirations as the daughter of a legal immigrant. But if we use our imagination, we can conjure up a better life for Isabelle, Medina, and all of us who strive to combine family and work with the assistance of our government and society.

In each chapter, we see that the uniquely American response to the needs of the worker and the family is sometimes justified under the rubric of laissez-faire capitalism—a capitalism that I believe should more aptly be termed *hypercapitalism*. This hypercapitalism is finally beginning to receive long-due criticism from sources as diverse as philanthropist-financier George Soros, who sounded the alarm in a 1997 *Atlantic Monthly* cover story;[1] to Robert Kuttner, whose critically acclaimed book, *Everything for Sale*, is subtitled the *Virtues and Limits of Markets;*[2] to the late Leonard Silk, economics reporter for the *New York Times* and *Newsweek*, a self-avowed capitalist who similarly questioned the unrelenting and single-minded manifestation of American capitalism after the cold war.[3]

This emerging critique, however, has not yet reached the U.S. Congress. A Republican Congress swept into office in 1992 proclaiming "laissez-faire" capitalism, even though their version of capitalism has little similarity to a pure laissez-faire model. They proposed rolling back federal regulatory power and reducing federal outlays from one-third to one-half in order to advance "the simple idea that people should be trusted to spend their own earnings and decide their own futures."[4] At the same time, Congress recommended increasing the federal military budget with its inefficient subsidy of industries. These proposals would supposedly help create a "just and compassionate society" but can easily be unmasked as corporate welfare at the expense of the working class. Although the Republican revolution was not entirely successful, it did push President Bill Clinton to endorse a welfare reform package that radically departs from our previous understanding of the relationship between the state and the family.

American-style capitalism helps perpetuate the class inequities among Americans while also undermining the interests of our economy as a whole. We cannibalize our most pre-

cious resource—the health and well-being of the next generation—to serve the interests of the ultrarich. Although American
politicians applaud such results in the name of laissez-faire economics, no other Western industrialized country—nor even
Adam Smith—would recognize these policies as laissez-faire.
The answer, however, is not to strive to turn American-style
capitalism into a purer laissez-faire model. The answer is to
introduce a moral component into American capitalism that
protects the most disadvantaged members of our society rather
than only the ultrarich. Such a capitalism dominates the legal-
economic landscape of Canada, western Europe, Great Britain,
and Australia to a greater extent than it does in the United
States.

Law schools and legal education in the United States often
disregard the legal-economic structures of other countries. The
proponents of the field labeled "law and economics" frequently
rely on a distorted version of laissez-faire economics and make
little reference to economic and legal systems outside those of
the United States. In the purported name of laissez-faire capitalism, they applaud the hodgepodge of inadequate protection
for American workers and families. Their distorted view of laissez-faire economics has also seeped into American legal decisions and statutory law.

The belief that government intervention in the workplace is
inherently inefficient greatly influences many judges on the
courts of appeals as well as the justices of the U.S. Supreme
Court. Why we should care more about the economic freedom
of entrepreneurs than the needs of workers is rarely addressed.
As Jules L. Coleman noted in a stinging critique of the economic
analysis of Judge Richard Posner's work, "[T]here is a difference
between saying—if you want to promote utility or wealth then

these are the rules you should adopt—and saying—because these rules would promote utility or wealth in the abstract we should adopt them."[5] But as a scholar and as a judge, Posner repeatedly assumes that a rule is appropriate simply because it maximizes utility or wealth.

American law needs a more humane economic basis. The prevailing economics in law must be exposed so that we can question America's mindless devotion to its hypercapitalism. What exactly is the American version of capitalism? Should it promote efficiency and utility at the expense of all other values? Or is it possible to maintain a private marketplace while also recognizing the inherent limitations of entrepreneurs as decision makers? Does American law consistently follow a laissez-faire approach to the workplace, or is it inconsistently laissez-faire, to the detriment of the most underprivileged members of our society? Why do we withdraw benefits from welfare moms under the assumption that they are lazy and selfish and, at the same time, increase benefits to middle-class parents under the assumption that they deserve more leisure time and economic assistance in order to be effective parents? And who is harmed by these policies—only the poor or the entire middle class? Finally, can we structure state intervention so that utility does not become selfishness and efficiency does not become greed?

This book does not challenge the inherent value of capitalism, however. Predictions that capitalism will inevitably self-destruct seem especially ill founded these days. Nearly every Western nation is based on a capitalist economy, and the few remaining Communist regimes continue to founder. Moreover, many Western countries are turning to the United States as an economic model and are considering abandoning their long-standing support of the family and worker. If there is one thing that we can safely predict, it is that the United States will remain firmly capitalistic and serve as a model for other countries trying to attain economic success.

Although the American version of capitalism is far from pure laissez-faire because it tolerates state intervention in the marketplace, the American version is generally less protective of the worker and family than are the versions used in other parts of the Western world. Not all kinds of capitalism, however, assume that utility and efficiency for the entrepreneurial class must be the dominant principles. Some favor the welfare of the worker out of the conviction that such policies benefit both workers and the economy as a whole. But the appropriateness of the American version of capitalism is rarely questioned in jurisprudence, perhaps because so little work on American law makes reference to other legal regimes.

Laissez-faire arguments are advanced in the United States most aggressively when lawmakers or activists seek to extend protections to the less privileged members of our society, and they are ignored when politicians and others recommend greater protection for middle-class Americans. American law reflects neither a laissez-faire economy nor a social welfare state; instead, it has a capitalistic perspective that disproportionately benefits the entrepreneurial class and often relies on a moralistic agenda.

Other countries provide a larger social safety net to families and workers, not simply out of a desire to achieve greater class equity, but from a conviction that such policies benefit all society. Today's child who receives nurturing care from parents who have been provided with health insurance and paid maternal or paternal leave will be tomorrow's responsible member of the community. But even though such programs benefit the long-term interests of society, it is unrealistic to expect employers to provide for free those benefits for the well-being of society. Rather, such decisions can be made only at a governmental level because "even in a market economy there are realms of human life where markets are imperfect, inappropriate, or unattainable."[6] Furthermore, the United States is virtually the only Western capitalist economy to leave the development of such policies primarily in the hands of entrepreneurs.

The point of this book is not that the United States should blindly adopt the policies of western European countries or Canada. Instead, the point is that a comparative investigation of the policies of other capitalist countries should lead us to modify our version of capitalism. By looking at examples of other capitalist economies, we can see the inequities and limitations of American capitalism. As I will show, even Adam Smith would give a failing grade to the economics underlying American law.

### Laissez-Faire Legal Economics

Although public interest law grew substantially in the 1970s and early 1980s with a sharp critique of the state's treatment of the poor, the last decade has brought a heightened interest in laissez-faire economic principles in law. Nearly every law school in the United States has added a course on law and economics to its curriculum. In some schools, this is even a required course in which students are taught how to apply economic principles to law, under the assumption that American law has—and should have—a laissez-faire, capitalistic perspective. The teaching materials in this area seldom offer any critique of this increasingly dominant philosophy, and in the meantime, the law of the welfare state has vanished from many law school curricula. As governmental assistance for society's less privileged members has become more unpopular, law schools have reorganized to focus on the law of the entrepreneurial class rather than the law of the poor. Students graduate from law school understanding the economics underlying the tax code (with its subsidies for the rich) but knowing nearly nothing about the economics underlying the new welfare laws.

The origins of law and economics in American law schools can be traced to Richard Posner, currently a judge on the U.S. Court of Appeals for the Seventh Circuit. In 1973, he published the first textbook treatise on the economic analysis of legal rules and institutions. Now in its fourth edition,[7] this book aspires to make his brand of law and economics the foundational principle for the entire legal system.

Unbalanced in the extreme, Posner's work presumes that the principles of value, utility, and efficiency should govern the analysis of law from an economic perspective based on the assumption that human behavior is rational. Acknowledging that a reader might have trouble with this view of human rationality, Posner offers some (unsubstantiated) generalizations about the predictive power of law and economics and concludes: "[S]o perhaps the assumption that people are rational maximizers of their satisfaction is not so unrealistic as the noneconomist might at first think."[8] Why we should choose the concepts of value, utility, and efficiency to measure the appropriateness of a particular set of laws is not something that Posner even cares to address.

Posner's work is parochial; he never refers to examples outside the United States, and much of his economic support is outdated as well. For example, in his brief discussion of Aid for Families with Dependent Children (AFDC), he states that such programs "have been found to have surprisingly large negative effects on participation in the labor force—in the case of AFDC, participation by mothers."[9] His sole support is a chapter written by Martin Anderson in a book published in 1978 in which Anderson summarizes previously completed studies of behavior in the United States. These "facts" are supposed to be sufficient to allow the reader to assess the efficiency of AFDC.

The actual relationship between AFDC benefits and the mothers of young children seeking paid employment is much more complicated than Posner suggests. Examination of the social welfare programs in the United States and France reveals that we must also weigh the efficiency of social welfare payments within the structure of all assistance provided to the state for mothers of young children.[10] France effectively integrates women into the paid labor force after their children reach the age of three, by offering a system of time-limited transfer payments along with a system of extensive support to working families through universal public day care, universal medical insurance, universal family allowances, and federally mandated maternity leave. These programs are not exclusively based on need. Rather, they were created out of a conviction that all children—rich and poor—benefit from developing nurturing relationships with their parents in the first several years of life.

The recently enacted Personal Responsibility and Work Opportunity Act incorporated one piece of the French system—time-limited transfer payments—without incorporating the broader picture of general state support for all families. The economic assumption underlying this change is that AFDC payments created a disincentive for poor single mothers to seek paid employment. Although time-limited transfer payments are supposed to eliminate this disincentive, without an accompanying social safety net, they are unlikely to achieve the effectiveness of the French model. Poor, single mothers will still be unlikely to pursue paid employment while their children are young. What are they to do with their children while they are at work? Can they expect to earn more than their child care, transportation, and medical costs (since their children will lose access to free medical care after their mother accepts employment in an uninsured industry)? And where are these jobs that they are supposed to be able to find? Should these people serve as domestic workers in other people's households while abandoning their own children during the day?

A comparative examination also reveals that U.S.law, despite its "profamily" rhetoric, is generally much less supportive of parenting than are the laws of other countries. We must wonder why U.S. policy is generally so determined to push the parents of young children into paid labor. In Sweden, incentives to mothers to join the paid labor force do not appear until the child reaches the age of eighteen months.[11] In France, incentives to enter the paid labor force are offered only after children reach the age of three. But the United States offers little support to any families (poor or middle class) for a parent to stay home to care for a child.

As a result, the United States has the highest rate of any country of labor force participation by young mothers, with the net result being a marked decline in their sleep and free time. On average, married, college-educated, working women with young children have seven fewer hours of passive leisure and sleep than do their male partners. One can only imagine the sleep deprivation of the many poor women who raise children on their own. The quality of life for women and their children, however, has no place in law and economics. In the name of efficiency, the United States encourages all adults to participate in the paid labor force while offering little state support for child care. The disproportionate negative consequences for the quality of life for women and their children receive scant attention.

Why should we as a society encourage parents of young children to enter the paid labor force in larger numbers? A common response is that we should be encouraging primary parents, who are disproportionately women, to return to the labor force in order to promote economic equality between women and men. Gaps in labor force participation arguably hurt women's economic earning power, although this response assumes that men's lives are the norm to which women should aspire. Alternatively, we could try to create policies that encourage fathers and mothers to spend equal amounts of time caring for their children. Instead of encouraging women to work without interruption, we could encourage men to interrupt their labor force participation. This solution would improve the quality of care available to children and also increase the primary parent's leisure time. It is a solution premised on the needs of all parents and their children, not just the parents and children of a particular socioeconomic class.

Most other Western countries have chosen to value the quality of life of women and children over their coerced entry into the paid labor force. Sweden, for example, has tried to create social and economic policies that help fathers spend more time with their children. Led by the unrealistic assumptions of law and economics, U.S. welfare policies contribute to the deterioration of the lives of women and children. Oddly, law and economics ignores the quality of our next generation as the external effect of this policy.

Readers who are interested in alternative perspectives on law and economics currently have few sources of guidance in law. Nearly all the published teaching materials are structured around considerations of efficiency and utility maximization, with no comparisons with other economic systems or jurisprudential perspectives.[12]

The only modest exception to this trend is a slim paperback by Robin Paul Malloy entitled *Law and Economics: A Comparative Approach to Theory and Practice*. This book's notion of "comparative" is to share with the reader a variety of theoretical perspectives that one might use in thinking about the connection between law and economics. It does not rely exclusively on a laissez-faire, capitalistic perspective but, instead, exposes the reader to liberalism, communitarianism, libertarianism, and other economic philosophies. Six pages are even devoted to critical legal theory, and other sections of the book attempt to reveal the ideological bias of conservative law and economics. All the cases that are chosen for the readers' examination, however, are from the United States and tend to reflect a laissez-faire view of law and economics. It is unlikely that students could offer a sophisticated critique of law and economics based on these scant materials.

As each of these books states in its preface or introduction, law and economics is an increasingly popular area of study in American law schools. Some believe that "law and economics is the most important development in the field of law in the last fifty years."[13] But what has not been said often enough is that this field is parochial and narrow in its consideration of the relationship between law and economics. In this book, I respond to the narrowness of the field by examining some core areas of American law in comparison with that of other countries to show how American law purports to favor laissez-faire policies while, in fact, protecting the rich at the expense of the quality of life for most members of our society. Rather than applaud the application of economic principles to law, I will show the inconsistent and morally offensive ways in which these principles have been applied to American law. It is time to add a discussion of fairness and equity to the study of law and economics rather than focus exclusively on efficiency and utility. The quality of our lives depends on it.

### Laissez-Faire Legal Decisions

Law and economics is not just an academic discipline. Judge Posner's ascendancy to the bench reflects its direct influence on the law. In the hands of conservative judges, principles of efficiency and utility are used to the disservice of all and especially the less privileged members of our society. The dramatic influence of these principles on law is documented throughout this book, but a few brief examples give a hint of their impact.

Justice Antonin Scalia enlists these principles to argue that the government should not be allowed to implement affirmative action programs because no group in society can claim to have been subjected to an acute disadvantaged status in the past that entitles it to preferential treatment today. In a racial reverse discrimination case brought by a white contractor against the city of Richmond, Virginia, Scalia wrote:

> The relevant proposition is not that it was blacks, or Jews, or Irish who were discriminated against, but that it was individual men and women, "created equal," who were discriminated against. . . . Racial preferences appear to "even the score" (in some small degree) only if one embraces the proposition that our society is appropriately viewed as divided into races, making it right that an injustice rendered

in the past to a black man should be compensated for by discriminating against a white. Nothing is worth that embrace.[14]

Similarly, in a gender reverse discrimination case brought by Paul Johnson, a male blue-collar worker, against a city transportation authority, Scalia argued that the state has no right to decide to protect the employment interests of Diane Joyce, a female blue-collar worker over Johnson at the defendant's workplace. On behalf of Johnson, Scalia noted: "The irony is that these individuals—predominantly unknown, unaffluent, unorganized—suffer this injustice at the hands of a Court fond of thinking itself the champion of the politically impotent."[15]

Justice Scalia's opinions consistently protect the affluent at the expense of the disadvantaged. For example, he would have been willing to allow the state of Virginia to maintain its exclusively male military college[16] (nevertheless in 1997, the Virginia Military Institute admitted women as part of its freshman class) while forbidding a transportation agency from providing the most modest preference to allow, for the first time, a female blue-collar worker to seek a supervisory position.[17] But why should the state of Virginia be allowed to privilege men over women who seek military training? Such a result is inefficient, presuming the inherent superiority of men over women. And certainly no coherent historical argument can be made that men need or deserve such special protection. Scalia's concern for fairness and efficiency enters his decisions only when the group challenging preferential treatment is white men. Scalia should be able to use his laissez-faire lens to see that it is inefficient for the government to deny military training opportunities to women under the stereotypical assumption that they are inherently unqualified for military service. It is not simply unfair to women to deny them these opportunities, but according to laissez-faire principles, the long-term interests of society suffer from such inefficient policies.

Judge Frank Easterbrook, who sits with Judge Posner on the Seventh Circuit, invoked the most striking statement of the efficiency principle, in an employment law case: "Greed is the foundation of much economic activity, and Adam Smith told us that each person's pursuit of his own interests drives the economic system to produce more and better goods and services for all."[18] Citing that principle, Easterbrook sided with an entrepreneur against a worker whose loyalty was demanded despite his employer's blatantly illegal behavior.

Easterbrook, like Scalia and Posner, however, misreads Adam Smith. Smith never romanticized the role of the state in the economy. Nor did he romanticize what we can expect from the entrepreneurial class. Rather, he propounded a laissez-faire perspective because he believed that the entrepreneurial class would try to dominate the state for its own benefit, and indeed, America's distorted invocation of laissez-faire economics has proved Smith to be largely correct. Even the courts are sometimes complicit in the conspiracy to aid the entrepreneurial class. In the hands of law and economics, we get the worst of laissez-faire economics—legal protection of only the entrepreneurial class—to the detriment of the long-term interests of society as a whole.

### Laissez-Faire Statutory Law

Although many parts of the 1995 Republican Congress's Contract with America were premised on laissez-faire capitalism, the Personal Responsibility and Work Opportunity Act, enacted in 1996, is the best example of its influence on American statutory law. This statute radically changed America's response to poor families by eliminating financial assistance as an entitlement. Federal assistance now is given to the states in the form of block grants that specify how this money can be allocated. The center-piece of the legislation is the requirement that assistance be time limited. Anyone who fails to find employment within a specified time period (usually two years) will be denied further assistance, even if that person is responsible for raising young children.

Children rights' advocates are holding their breath, waiting to find out what the consequences for America's children will be. At first, Speaker of the House Newt Gingrich suggested that more children could enter orphanages, proceeding from his naive assumption that orphanages are healthy and economical places in which to raise children. (One wonders, given Gingrich's antigovernment sentiments, why he believes that the government should pay people to take care of children in orphanages rather than provide financial assistance to parents so that they can raise their own children.) It is now generally assumed that foster care may have to deal with the overflow children, since foster care assistance has not (yet) been included as part of the states' block grants. (It is still part of the federal budget's "entitlements.")

Increasing the expenditures for foster care while decreasing the expenditures for welfare, however, does not square with all laissez-faire economists. Some laissez-faire proponents object to any state intervention on behalf of children, including state support for foster care. When confronted with the dire consequences of such an approach, however, one free-market economist was forced to admit that "of course, some children will die" while their parents tried to learn the lessons of free-market economics and limit the production of children.[19] This apparently is an acceptable result in a system in which laissez-faire economics is the only recognized value. The long-term interests of our children is irrelevant.

Although other countries have used time-limited assistance to poor families, no other Western country has tried to do so within a system of extreme laissez-faire capitalism. Instead, they have created effective programs that nearly guarantee employment to parents after their youngest child reaches the age of two or three. Cash assistance is eliminated because other programs, like state-subsidized child care and job training, have taken their place. These programs target all parents out of the conviction that the state is responsible for safeguarding the health and well-being of the next generation.

An overview of governmental intervention into the lives of workers and the family can reveal the values that underlie American social policy. American law benefits the interests of a small elite in American society. That is, American law has two tiers. Programs of social insurance like Social Security are valued highly in the United States, and programs of social assistance like AFDC are disparaged. A comprehensive review of American social policy shows that middle-class men and women who conform to traditional gender roles often benefit under American social policy at the expense of other, less valued individuals and families. Although these "others"—racial minorities, poor people, single mothers, and gays and lesbians—constitute a majority of people in our society, American social policy is often trapped in a nineteenth-century conception of society that "fit[s] and reinforce[s] the family wage system, with men as breadwinners and women as primary caretakers, domestic workers and secondary wage earners."[20] It is time to move into the twenty-first century with a more flexible understanding of the family and the individual person, with social programs that satisfy this social reality.

## Capitalism Is Not Capitalism Is Not Capitalism

The U.S. Constitution was based on a particular brand of capitalism—that of Adam Smith[21]—with its laissez-faire expectations that the government would not interfere with the private ownership of capital. Hence, the Fifth Amendment to the U.S. Constitution protects people's right to own and control private property.

Adam Smith's model has little in common with the current Gingrich-style economic model. Smith's objection to government interference in the economy rested on the assumption that merchants would control government and thereby impose restraints that would serve their self-interest. He worried that government interference in the marketplace "unchains the selfishness of humanity and permits it to do harm to the community rather than working for the public benefit."[22] Smith "feared monopoly power far more than he feared unwarranted government intervention in the market mechanism."[23] Smith lived in the days of robber barons and worried about their monopoly influence on government and society. If the government had not been a government of merchants but instead represented the working people, Smith might not have been as opposed to governmental intervention in the workplace. It is wrong, therefore, to use Smith's philosophy as an excuse to undermine the limited protections legislated on behalf of workers and the family. Yet while purporting to draw on the work of Adam Smith, modern American capitalism has not been willing to use the state as a weapon against the selfishness of the merchant class. Instead, American law is premised on the assumption that welfare moms, not entrepreneurs, are selfish.

American hypercapitalism mirrors the evils that concerned Adam Smith. Its intervention often does the greatest disservice to the most underprivileged members of our society. For example, if we look more closely at government intervention in the workplace, we see that the most disadvantaged workers—domestic and agricultural workers—are usually excluded from coverage. When President Clinton had trouble finding a nominee for attorney general who had complied with the minimal protections provided by Social Security law for domestic employees, Congress reacted by broadening the exclusion (for the benefit of the upper class) without even considering its impact on domestic workers. The much-heralded Family and Medical Leave Act applies only to those workers who can afford to take unpaid leave and also happen to work for the 5 percent of American corporations that employ more than fifty employees.

Meanwhile, by reducing cash payments and imposing time limitations on benefits, the new welfare law makes it even more difficult for poor women to choose to stay home and care for their young children. This is treatment blatantly preferential to the upper class in contrast to the poor. (I say upper class rather than middle class because it is generally only the upper class that can afford to pay for the services of domestic workers or take extended unpaid leaves from work. The needs of the middle class for universal health insurance, government-subsidized childcare, and paid parenting leave have not been addressed by Congress or the president.) If such policies that disproportionately benefit the upper class are the inevitable result of laissez-faire economics, then one must question the morality of laissez-faire economics. If such policies are not inevitable, then they should be noted and changed to create a more equitable society. No other Western industrialized nation tips the balance so far against the interests of the poor and the middle class as the United States does.

Some economists—whose work is ignored by conservative law and economics—have a more realistic assessment of the way in which the economy works. The British economist John Maynard Keynes, for example, did not accept the premise that unemployment for qualified workers was antithetical to capitalism. Nor did he accept the premise that wages were determined entirely rationally under a capitalist system. Nonetheless, American law is based primarily on assumptions contrary to how the "economy in which we live actually works."[24]

Academic economists have carefully explored the validity of those assumptions on which proponents of laissez-faire economics rely. They have concluded that there is no evidence that social protection programs negatively affect the labor market's flexibility or the speed of the labor market's adjustment. In addition, they have concluded that the absence of social protection policies—like mandatory health insurance—does have a negative impact on people's well-being.[25] In other words, government intervention in the workplace can serve the long-term interests of all society. Law and economics is wrong to assume that government intervention in the private marketplace necessarily detracts from the efficiency of the market.

Similarly, academic economists have disputed the Republicans' claim that "welfare spending and other forms of social protection inevitably lead to inefficient allocation of resources and undermine economic growth."[26] The social market economies of northern Europe have consistently produced higher gross domestic products (GDP) than the United States' or Great Britain's economy has. Although one might argue that these economies would have operated even better had they used more laissez-faire principles, the evidence does not support this claim. Social market arrangements have actually facilitated wage restraint as well as contributed to economic efficiency and growth through worker training and other investments in human capital. The United States has not facilitated long-term investment in human capital through social market protection. If our choices were based on a careful study of the experience of other countries rather than unexamined rhetoric, we might make different and more humane choices. We might make choices that benefit both workers and the long-term interests of society.

It is possible to incorporate human values into capitalism by providing basic rights to workers. Canada, Australia, and various European countries have attempted to structure their societies based on that understanding. (Great Britain appears once again to be in a transition—away from [Milton] Friedman-like economics and back toward Keynes.) Recent U.S. statutory law accompanied by narrow interpretations of that law, however, has made such a reconciliation virtually impossible. It is time to learn from our trading partners who have managed to combine healthy capitalistic economies with basic protections for workers. Only in the parochial literature of law and economics does laissez-faire capitalism exist in the United States. But other versions of capitalism are well accepted by academic economists and are thriving in countries outside the United States.

### The Future

Law and economics often presumes that a free market with little or no state intervention is in society's best interest because a free market best allows workers and owners to use their human capital. But an employee who is identifiable as a member of a racial minority group may not be given an opportunity to demonstrate his or her abilities. Similarly, a person's disability, family responsibilities, or pregnancy may make it difficult for him or her to participate effectively in the labor market. Does capitalism mean that we must structure our employment rules under the assumption that those problems do not really exist or that they are relatively unimportant? Or can capitalism incorporate an understanding of these problems and develop an effective response? Finally, is it even fair to describe American capitalism as evenhandedly following a laissez-faire model?

The United States need not abandon capitalism to provide appropriate protections for employees at the workplace. But citizens and workers in the United States are often unaware of the choices available in capitalism. Capitalism need not be based on assumptions contrary to the world in which we live. As in Canada and much of western Europe, capitalism can be based on the understanding that workers face arbitrary discrimination, disability and illness, and child care and family responsibilities. The law of employment can make capitalism operate more efficiently by enabling employees to shoulder these responsibilities effectively rather than denying that these responsibilities are commonplace for most American workers. A humane capitalism should be possible.

To develop such a capitalism in the United States, we need to expand the voices that are considered to include those schooled in the practical implications of law and social policy. Economist Alan Enhrehalt argues that such voices are crucial to this discussion because they do not rely on unrealistic postulates borrowed from theoretical economics:

Market economics enshrines choice and lionizes the individual. Carried to its furthest extreme, it all but suggests that anything the individual really feels like doing can't be wrong. . . . As the mantra for millions of Americans, perhaps most of a generation, this set of ideas is entitled to some respect. But it need not be taken at face value, and mastery of algebra should not be a prerequisite for discussing it.[27]

This book describes the economics that underlies American law, but without formulas or charts. The picture that it paints is taken from the real world in which we live, not from a set of assumptions about the behavior of fictional humans. We must examine this picture closely if we are to create a more humane capitalism. Only then will Isabelle's side of the story be reflected in our national policies concerning workers and families.

# 2

## AFFIRMATIVE ACTION

In the eighteenth century, upper-class Boston families could send their nearly illiterate children to Harvard University.[1] Until the 1920s, admission to elite institutions often was restricted to those males who could afford to pay the tuition and had taken courses generally only available in private schools such as Latin.[2] Today, money continues to buy privilege in the United States. Despite the extent of economic privilege in American society, we continue to cling to the myth of equal opportunity, viewing the notion of economic privilege "as a radical, dangerous idea, or an idiosyncratic throwback to the past, conjuring up countries with monarchies, nobility, serfs, and peasants."[3]

In the late twentieth century, some institutions of higher education instituted affirmative action programs for some members of racial minorities (all the while continuing their policy of alumni preference for privileged whites). But affirmative action has and continues to receive much criticism, with the result of stigmatizing its beneficiaries. When upper-class members of society receive benefits, no one notices, but when minority members receive benefits, everyone notices and criticizes these benefits. In 1985 Harvard University President Derek Bok commented on this distinction when he asked why whites resent affirmative action for blacks but do not express "similar resentments against other groups of favored applicants, such as athletes and alumni offspring."[4]

Embedded in the affirmative action debate are two assumptions—that affirmative action means that unqualified, or less qualified, persons are selected over more qualified individuals and that a negative relationship exists between affirmative action and workforce productivity.[5] In other words, the principles of laissez-faire capitalism reinforce the backlash against affirmative action on behalf of disadvantaged groups in the United States while condoning affirmative action for privileged members of our society. "Affirmative action for the children of Founding Fathers just doesn't seem to carry the stigma."[6]

Laissez-faire capitalism helps maintain American law's hypocritical perspective on affirmative action and helps propertied whites gain access to educational institutions or employment settings while criticizing comparable devices that support African Americans. Hiding behind laissez-faire capitalism, with its emphasis on efficiency and personal autonomy, this field of law reflects disturbing stereotypical attitudes toward race. Efficiency and personal autonomy are cited only when racial minorities or women seek societal protection; such concepts rarely are used to question societal protection for white males.

## Anti-Affirmative Action Economics

The dogma of efficiency has selectively infiltrated the law of discrimination. Richard Posner argues that an affirmative action program designed to achieve a proportional representation of racial minorities at institutions of higher education is inefficient because it distorts the results of preexisting personal preferences: "[T]his sort of intervention would, by profoundly distorting the allocation of labor and by driving a wedge between individual merit and economic and professional success, greatly undermine the system of incentives on which a free society depends."[7]

The dogma of personal autonomy has permitted Richard Epstein to question the validity of the government's authorizing or requiring affirmative action for a subgroup of society:

> There is no external measure of value that allows the legal system or the public at large to impose its preferences on the parties in their own relationship. There is thus no reason to have to decide whether we should weigh the need for merit in employment decisions against the need for diversity in workers.[8]

Similarly, Posner contends that affirmative action on behalf of racial minorities has "no logical stopping point" short of a standard of "perfect equality."[9] The government interferes with personal autonomy when it imposes on employers its views of which subgroups are entitled to affirmative action.

Posner's concern for efficiency appears to wane, however, when such arguments are used to support race-based affirmative action. It might be efficient, for example, to offer race-based preferences to help an entire class of people overcome decades of entrenched poverty. But when confronted with such an argument, Posner backs away from his overarching concern for efficiency: "To say that discrimination is often a rational and efficient form of behavior is not to say that it is socially or ethically desirable."[10] Even if race-based affirmative action is the most efficient way to achieve socioeconomic equality, Posner asserts that given the costs of acquiring individualized information, we should not permit the state's use of race-based categories. At this point, Posner becomes a staunch formal equality or "color-blind" theorist, arguing that we must not confuse what is "efficient" with what is "good" or "right."

Posner's occasional recitation of formal equality principles, however, is inconsistent with his use elsewhere of the personal autonomy principle. A formal equality theorist believes that the government must not permit the private marketplace to deviate from race-blind principles when creating policies even if private actors sincerely believe that race-conscious policies are necessary, for example, to overcome centuries of racial subordination. This view is inconsistent with the personal autonomy principle because it permits the moral principle of formal equality to trump an employer's autonomy interests in defining his or her own hiring policies. By hiding behind the purported principle of efficiency, Posner and other theorists can selectively support some governmental policies while criticizing others. These inconsistent strands of law and economics have created a patchwork of case law that disserve the interests of African Americans desiring access to higher education or employment in the workplace.

## Educational Affirmative Action

Educational institutions of higher education have never relied exclusively on the "merit" principle in deciding whom to admit.

Until the 1920s, the only "merit" requirement was that applicants take a list of courses available only at private schools. These requirements, however, soon came under attack because they allowed immigrant Jews and Catholics to enter these elite institutions. Harvard President A. Lawrence Lowell tried to respond to this problem in the 1920s by imposing a ceiling on the number of Jews admitted, but he backed down from this proposal when he received a barrage of public criticism. Instead, he established an alumni preference policy that discriminated against children of immigrants, many of whom were Jewish or Catholic. Lowell therefore used an indirect rather than a direct method of discrimination. As a result of this policy, at least a quarter of Harvard's entering classes were the sons of graduates, a figure that has remained relatively stable ever since.[11]

Although Harvard has presumably discontinued its practice of overtly discriminating against Jewish or Catholic applicants, it has never discontinued its preference for alumni. This policy offers the children of alumni a procedural and substantive advantage in the admissions process. Procedurally, all other applications go to an admissions committee for review before reaching the desk of the dean of admissions. The applications of children of alumni, however, go directly to the dean of admissions for reading. The dean then writes such comments on the file as "Not a great profile but just strong enough #'s and grades to get the tip from lineage."[12] The alumni preference is clearly a "preference": between 1983 and 1992, an admitted nonlegacy candidate, on average, scored thirty-five points higher than did an admitted legacy candidate.

Whereas racial minorities are often accused of obtaining an unfair advantage in the admissions process, legacy candidates are given an equal or greater advantage. In 1988, for example, approximately two hundred applicants received alumni prefer-ence—a figure that exceeded the total number of blacks, Mexi-can Americans, Puerto Ricans, and Native Americans enrolled in the freshman class.

The legacy preference was originally introduced to discrimi-nate against recent immigrant groups, such as Jews and Catholics. Today, it has a disparate impact on Asian Americans and other minority groups that are unlikely to be able to take advantage of an alumni preference. In response to a discrimina-tion complaint filed by Asian American applicants to Harvard University, the Office of Civil Rights of the U.S. Department of Education concluded that alumni preference, coupled with a preference for athletes, created a higher admission rate for white applicants over similarly qualified Asian American applicants. (Nonetheless, their complaint was found to be without merit.)

In the 1970s, elite American universities began to change their admissions policies to present an image of more racial, eth-nic, religious, and geographic diversity. Many institutions that historically had been restricted to white men were opened to women and various racial minorities. Despite these changes, however, some remnants of earlier admissions practices remained in place, and new ones were added. Alumni preference continued to benefit a subset of whites, although for the first time, female applicants could benefit from this preference. (At state schools, political connections rather than alumni prefer-ence were often favored.)[13] Athletic preferences helped male athletes who, at some institutions like Harvard, were also pre-dominantly white.

A new admission policy that emerged in this time period was increased reliance on grades and especially test scores. Whereas graduation from elite secondary schools and an ability to pay the tuition were the sole admissions criteria before the 1920s, the post-World War II era saw the emergence of so-called merit criteria of grades and test scores. In the 1960s, when scholarships eventually became available for students from impoverished backgrounds, many African Americans were still unable to attend elite institutions because of these recently invoked "merit" criteria.

Admissions testing originally began as an attempt to help make threshold judgments about candidates' abilities to succeed. Over time, however, these tests evolved "from a threshold to a relative measure" and, in turn, led to the disproportionate rejection of African American applicants at exactly the time they became formally eligible for admission and financial aid.[14] By the 1970s, competitive admissions testing became standard at nearly all institutions of legal education.[15] Today, it is estimated that only 5.9 percent of college-bound high school seniors can meet the competitive criteria used by elite institutions, with only 0.4 percent of college-bound African American seniors meeting these criteria.[16]

What merit criteria do these tests seek to measure? Early attacks by minority groups on the LSAT (Law School Admission Test) focused on the test's inability to predict success in law school. The empirical evidence suggested that the tests predicted success equally for minority and majority students, although it was not a particularly good predictor for either group. Because no evidence of predictive inequality was found, "this significant flaw [in its predictability for any group] was lost in the pressure to have some testing instrument."[17] Also lost in the debate was how important it was to predict first-year grades in law school as a criterion for admissions, rather than success in the profession.[18] The obsession with testing that began to overtake American culture in the 1970s therefore caused institutions to be blind to the accuracy or relevance of testing while also discounting the significance of the impact against racial minorities.

Even when institutions attempt to diversify their student body, they almost never abandon their prime reliance on grades and test scores. As Derrick Bell eloquently argued: "The decision to maintain grades and test scores as the prime criteria for admission advantages the upper class and ensures that the nation's economically privileged will continue to occupy the great majority of the highly sought-after seats in prestigious colleges, medical, and law schools."[19]

In the 1970s, therefore, two divergent transformations took place in American thinking about admissions to educational institutions. On the one hand, Americans increasingly believed that admissions were based largely on "merit," placing great weight on the reliability of standardized tests to evaluate it. On the other hand, Americans began to believe that racial minorities were the only group sometimes to gain admissions without meeting such objective criteria. "While tirades against affirmative action regularly fill the pages of magazines and newspapers, the most disturbing form of affirmative action—preference given to children of alumni, known as 'legacies'—is usually ignored by critics."[20] Only racial minorities were targeted as a group undeserving of admissions on merit grounds alone. Minority students do not have the political or academic connections to provide the support network of the preferentially admitted majority students.[21]

Minority group members were singled out as receiving "preferential" treatment, but majority group members, who were even more likely to have been given preferential treatment, were not subject to criticism or stigma. One might sim-

ply say that various criteria were used for admissions purposes—test scores, parents' educational status, political connections, talent in male sports, and race. One would not necessarily label any of them as more or less appropriate or problem-
atic. Yet American society cleverly groups these criteria along
racist lines, not questioning the criteria that benefit whites and
males but questioning those criteria that benefit racial minorities. When the Office of Civil Rights investigated whether Harvard's use of legacy preference discriminated against Asian
American applicants, the office upheld Harvard's use of the
legacy preference despite its adverse impact, because these
preferences were "long-standing and legitimate." Alumni preference is thus defended as an appropriate organizational principle, whereas race-based affirmative action comes under
increased attack.

The point here is not to argue that race-based affirmative
action is entirely good or that alumni preference is entirely bad.
Rather, the point is that the public perception of admissions
policies is filtered through a racist lens. When the group that is
targeted for assistance shifts from a predominantly white male
economic elite to an African American subclass, the public takes
notice and complains about the derogation of the merit principle. There is no uniformly applied merit principle operating in
American society. Instead, a merit myth is invoked when the
color of the beneficiary group starts to darken.

Laissez-faire economics has played a role in this inconsistent
development of the law of preferential treatment. The case that
best captures this role is *Hopwood v. State of Texas*.[22] Relying
on the scholarship of Richard Posner, the Fifth Circuit over-
turned a racial criterion in admissions while affirming a preference for whites. It concluded that a university may not consider

an individual's race in the application process but can consider an applicant's "relationship to school alumni."

The alumni factor is a blatant preference for whites; to wit, the University of Texas excluded blacks from consideration for admission until 1950.[23] As recently as 1971 the University of Texas School of Law admitted no black students. Almost every child of every alumni from that year is white, but in the name of formal equality, the Fifth Circuit approved an alumni preference while disapproving a minority racial preference. In concluding that affirmative action does not even serve the interests of racial minorities, who are its targeted beneficiaries, the Fifth Circuit cited a 1974 law review article by Richard Posner that made unsubstantiated claims about the stigma against racial minorities. The article entirely ignored the body of scholarship since 1974 on the subject of stigma, and it never questioned why alumni children do not suffer from stigma due to their preferential treatment.

"Never have white judges, relying exclusively on the work of white scholars, spoken so authoritatively about the black experience in America," said Professor Leland Ware in criticizing the decision of the Fifth Circuit Court of Appeals in *Hopwood v. State of Texas.*[24]

Rather than focus on extensive scholarship by racial minorities concerning stigma, the Fifth Circuit relied exclusively on scholarship by whites. Richard Posner's 1974 law review article on the *DeFunis* case was cited three times with approval by the court, but a request by the Thurgood Marshall Legal Society and the Black Pre-Law Association to intervene was denied. Posner's work established the proposition (which these predominantly black organizations were not permitted to attempt to contradict) that "[t]he use of a racial characteristic to establish a presump-

tion that the individual also possesses other, and socially relevant, characteristics exemplifies, encourages, and legitimizes the
mode of thought and behavior that underlies most prejudice and
bigotry in modern America."[25] Why, then, didn't alumni children also face such prejudice and bigotry?

Posner's conjecture about prejudice, having been uttered in
1974 without empirical support, became a settled fact more than
twenty years later when quoted by the Fifth Circuit. Had the
court quoted black scholars like Randall Kennedy, they instead
would have had to deal with sophisticated responses like, "[t]he
problem with this view [that affirmative action entrenches
racial divisiveness] is that intense white resentment has accompanied every effort to undo racial subordination no matter how
careful the attempt to anticipate and mollify the reaction."[26] As
for the stigma argument, Professor Kennedy responds: "In the
end, the uncertain extent to which affirmative action diminishes
the accomplishments of blacks must be balanced against the
stigmatization that occurs when blacks are virtually absent from
important institutions in the society. . . . This positive result of
affirmative action outweighs any stigma that the policy
causes."[27]

Why, one must wonder, was Judge Posner's 1974 law review
cited as an authority on the effects of affirmative action on our
society, rather than Professor Kennedy's 1986 law review article, which also discusses the issue in "cost-benefit" terms? If
Posner is correct, why do so many African Americans support
affirmative action? Are they just plain stupid? Or are they as
smart as white alumni in recognizing the value of a degree from
a well-respected institution, regardless of the admissions criteria? The importance of the *Hopwood* opinion is that it makes
clear what earlier one might have been able only to suggest cyn-

ically—that law and economics' supposed concern for efficiency and personal autonomy is deployed in a way that disproportionately serves the interests of propertied whites.

Let us pretend for a moment that alumni preferences were held to the same strict scrutiny standard as racial preferences. Under the Constitution, policies that are subjected to strict scrutiny must meet a means/end justification. The ends that they seek to accomplish must be "compelling," and the means used to achieve those ends must be narrowly tailored to achieve those ends. If alternative means are available to attain the stated objective that can avoid using the tainted category— in this case, alumni preference—then those alternative means must be used. In the language of law and economics, we should not permit the use of an inefficient criterion—alumni status— as a proxy for another characteristic that we want to measure. We should insist on using highly accurate indicators. Employing such reasoning with respect to the racial criterion, the Fifth Circuit says that it is offensive to use a racial preference as a proxy for another characteristic, such as diversity of viewpoint, because the preference does not meet the narrowly tailored portion of the constitutional standard. We should seek to use criteria that more perfectly match the characteristic that we purport to measure in order to better attain the stated objective.

Under this standard of efficiency, we cannot justify the alumni preference if it is being used inefficiently as a proxy for another characteristic, such as donations or academic excellence. Donations can be directly measured; no proxy is necessary or efficient. Moreover, giving weight to alumni giving contradicts the stated admissions criteria that are supposed to be "need blind." How can a process be need blind while also giving weight to alumni children, because of its beneficial effect on fund-raising? If we justify the legacy preference on a financial basis, then "it might save time and trouble simply to sell diplomas for their children to rich alumni parents through the mail."[28]

Academic excellence is often used to justify this preference. Harvard's dean of admissions, William Fitzsimmons, justified the preference in 1991 by stating that "[c]hildren of alumni are just smarter; they come from privileged backgrounds and tend to grow up in homes where parents encourage learning."[29] The empirical evidence, however, does not support this claim, since on average, these admittees have lower grades and test scores than do nonlegacy admittees. In addition, the standard measures of excellence (grades and test scores) probably already overstate the abilities of this group because they are likely to have had the economic resources to maximize their performance on these measures. In any event, the equation of alumni children with superior academic excellence (beyond the predictions that would otherwise be made from grades and test scores) is not logical, rational, or efficient. The last time that Harvard compared the performance of legacy and nonlegacy classmates was in 1956 when a study "showed Harvard sons hogging the bottom of the grade curve."[30]

Alternatively, one might argue that the alumni preference is not intended to stand as a proxy for something else, that it stands for itself, that a university preferentially values the children of its alumni because of their previous experience as children of alumni at that institution. Those children have something in common—they have grown up in a household in which one of the parents graduated from that institution. It is true that the composition of this group has been socially constructed.

One is not inherently—biologically—an alumni child; one becomes an alumni child because of something that one's parent has done either before or after one's birth. One then acquires this trait through one's parent.

But how valuable is a group identity that has existed for possibly only one generation? And does being the child of an alumnus or alumna really shape his or her identity in any meaningful way? Can it meet a compelling state interest standard? It is hard to justify an alumni preference that comes close to establishing a compelling, or even strong, state interest. Legacy preferences are simply affirmative action for the rich, pure and simple, with no noble purpose.[31] In the language of law and economics, there is no objective basis for this preference.

Justifications for racial affirmative action are, in fact, much stronger. As with the alumni category, it is now commonly acknowledged that race is a socially constructed experience. Anthropologically, racial differences among humans do not genuinely exist. But historically, we have created a meaning for certain characteristics that we label *race*. The social construction of those traits makes them no less real. An institution might value having someone present at a university who grew up identified as a member of a particular racial group. And unlike the alumni preference, this form of self-identity may have been passed on for many generations and learned at an early age. The views of the members of this group need not be identical in order for their presence to be valuable or noteworthy. In fact, the differences in their viewpoints might help rebut social stereotypes such as "all blacks think alike." But their presence reflects the reality of a genuine social category.

When he spoke about the effect on prejudice and bigotry, Posner misunderstood the justification for more than token participation by a racial minority group at an institution. The point is not that all blacks think alike, and so we do not need more blacks to attain diversity in viewpoint. Rather, the point is that all blacks do *not* think alike, but this fact will not be apparent until more than a token number of blacks attend an institution.

Posner is fond of reciting formal equality arguments to overturn affirmative action, but it is misleading to suggest that the law of educational admissions is really formally equal. Alumni preference policies are not subject to judicial challenge, despite their disparate impact against racial minorities, because disparate impact theory under the Constitution or Title VI of the Civil Rights Act of 1964 requires proof of "intent" to discriminate racially, which the courts have ruled is not available in such situations. Hence, the Office of Civil Rights ruled against the Asian American complainants in the racial discrimination case against Harvard University that challenged alumni preferences. Even though a disparate impact against Asian Americans may have existed, no direct evidence of intent to exclude Asian Americans was found. The historical evidence that alumni preference was originally created to exclude other immigrant groups—Jews and Catholics—was considered sufficient evidence of lawful intent. Racial preference policies for racial minorities, however, are subject to judicial challenge because they purportedly harm whites intentionally. Formal equality results in unequal justice when whites are given preference and blacks are not. Posner's version of law and economics requires blacks to justify the obvious benefits of more than token diversity (without considering black scholarship) and permits whites to perpetuate segregation without justification. This is not formal equality; it is the maintenance of a white, propertied social and economic structure.

## Employment Affirmative Action

Particular employment decisions, like particular educational admissions decisions, require that the criteria for selection be specified. In the employment area, such criteria are often considered to be based on merit unless they involve race-based affirmative action. Nonetheless, many of these criteria benefit whites, even though they do not correlate significantly with the capacity to perform the job in question. The criteria that disproportionately favor whites include word-of-mouth recruiting, high school or college diploma requirements, and "general intelligence" tests. When challenged as giving an unfair advantage to nonblack candidates for employment, these devices are often applauded by law and economics theorists despite little evidence of fairness or efficiency. By contrast, when any system is imposed to favor a black candidate for employment, these same theorists criticize the preference by hiding behind concerns for formal equality.

These employment criteria have not been consistent over time. Standardized testing is a twentieth-century phenomenon that began to be commonplace in civil service employment as overt race and gender barriers were eliminated. Such tests are presumed to test an applicant's ability to perform a job when in fact, both their predictive ability and their ability to compare candidates is limited.[32] As blacks came to have more schooling in the 1970s, a college education became increasingly important, although the actual value of a college degree is often presumed rather than empirically established. By 1980, the average black person had 12.0 years of school, compared with 12.5 years for whites, but fell behind in college education. In 1980, 17.1 percent of whites had received college diplomas, compared with only 8.4 percent of blacks.[33]

Whites have the opportunity to benefit from examination and education requirements, regardless of whether those criteria correlate with positive workplace performance. American culture simply presumes such a correlation. For example, when Epstein defends educational requirements, he does not rely on empirical evidence. Instead, he refers to the "global social perception that education, like good personal habits, is always job related."[34] And as is typical of such assertions, Richard Epstein relies on the work of Richard Posner to support his statement. Posner, in turn, based his correlation on "judicial and professional experience with educational requirements in law enforcement."[35] In fact, the courts that have examined the empirical evidence concerning educational requirements have not shared Judge Posner's presumption or conclusion.[36] Hence, as in the *Hopwood* case, such presumptions have been created by Richard Posner's unsubstantiated scholarship. As Randall Kennedy asked, "Would anyone claim that Henry Ford II was head of the Ford Motor Company because he was the most qualified person for the job?"[37]

One area of employment that is often considered meritocratic but is based on a history of exclusionary tactics is admission to the legal bar. In the early nineteenth century, admission standards were greatly reduced to permit nearly any eligible man to practice law.[38] Women and blacks were, of course, formally excluded from the practice of law.[39] When the American Bar Association unknowingly admitted three black lawyers to membership in 1912, it immediately passed a resolution precluding further associational miscegenation, thus ensuring its "lily-white membership for the next half-century."[40]

By the late nineteenth century, this practice began to come under attack when articles complained that "horde upon horde" were "connected with the practice of so noble a profession."[41] It was at this time that Christopher Columbus Langdell's views of legal education began to dominate American culture. Two explanations for Langdell's influence on the profession are his ties to Harvard and his "scientific" justification of legal education. The elitist values of law and economics that emerged during the Industrial Revolution were partly responsible for the development of more formal standards for admission to the bar. In 1921 and again in 1971, the American Bar Association approved the bar examination as a criterion for admission to the bar. Today, only the state of Wisconsin relies on the diploma privilege for bar admission, eschewing the bar examination. Hence, reliance on the bar examination for admission to the bar is a phenomenon of the late twentieth century. The role of the legal bar to weed out the "hordes" who wanted to practice law also was an expression of overt class bias. This class bias persists today as "bar associations tend to concentrate on low-status attorneys who have committed improprieties, turning a blind eye to the abuses of name partners at prestigious firms."[42]

In the eighteenth and nineteenth centuries, formal barriers excluded African Americans and women from the practice of law, whereas today, the bar exam disproportionately excludes African Americans from the practice of law. Although one cannot prove directly that the examination requirement was created to weed out African Americans, circumstantial evidence does support this view. For example, the state of South Carolina eliminated the diploma privilege and instituted the bar examination requirement exactly three years after the state opened its first black law school.[43] Then the "reading the bar" rule was eliminated in 1957, shortly after a black applicant used this method to gain admission. The state of South Carolina, of course, defends each of these changes on race-neutral grounds. Similarly, in Philadelphia, applicants for admission to the bar were photographed, and black applicants were seated side by side in the same row "to facilitate the grading of their examinations."[44] The racially conscious grading of the bar examination followed a covertly discriminatory preceptorship and registration system under which not a single black was admitted to the Pennsylvania bar between 1933 and 1943. Hence, the bar exam (with its racial impact) is of recent vintage in the United States.

The bar exam persists as a selection device, despite its disparate impact, because it is thought to weed out incompetent applicants to the bar. There is no evidence, however, that the bar exam tests one's ability to be a lawyer; instead, it is essentially an achievement test. It simply verifies a student's prior privilege "that [has] already been tested for at least three times in a law student's career, namely, during undergraduate training, the LSAT, and law school training."[45] Recognizing the correlation between grades in law school and passage of the bar examination, the Fourth Circuit stated: "An applicant for the Bar who has graduated from an accredited law school arguably may be said to stand before the Examiners armed with law school grades demonstrating that he possesses sufficient job-related skills. Why, then, any bar examination at all?"[46]

If the bar exam were required to withstand a rigorous standard of justification, it is doubtful that it would pass muster. Commenting on the selection of a cutoff passing score on the bar exam, for example, the Fourth Circuit noted: "We tend to agree with appellants' expert that, if this second system is utilized in the precise manner described by the Bar Examiners, it would be almost a matter of pure luck if the '70' thereby derived corresponded with anybody's judgment of minimal competence."[47] And when upholding the constitutionality of the bar exam under a very lenient constitutional standard, the Fourth Circuit acknowledged: "That is not to say that such an unprofessional approach leaves us with much confidence in the precise numerical results obtained." Despite the apparent imprecision of the bar examination, it persists as the predominant selection device. Its continued use reflects the Langdellian trend toward trying to introduce scientific principles into the selection of lawyers, regardless of the validity of those principles.

The bar exam is a uniquely American phenomenon. Other countries often require prospective lawyers to "article" in order to gain experience practicing law before being allowed to work on their own. But they do not rely on an invalidated multiple-choice exam to test students' substantive knowledge of law and also to exclude a distinct portion of those who have graduated from law school. In the United States, although Wisconsin does not require a bar exam for individuals who have graduated from a state institution, no one has complained about the relative competency of lawyers in that state. The modern persistence of the bar exam thus represents a state-sanctioned intrusion into the workplace that cannot be justified on efficiency grounds.

Ironically, when the law tries to force employers to justify examination or education requirements, scholars in the field of law and economics complain loudly. The case that exemplifies this phenomenon is *Griggs v. Duke Power*,[48] which was decided under Title VII of the Civil Rights Act of 1964 rather than under the Constitution. As in the bar examination example, *Griggs* is an excellent demonstration of how educational and testing requirements change as overt entry barriers to blacks are eliminated. In *Griggs*, an employer changed the rules for promotion from laborer-level jobs into higher-level jobs on the very day that Title VII went into effect (July 2, 1965). For the first time, employees were required to pass a high school equivalency program in order to be promoted. Their performance could be confirmed only by earning a set score on the Wonderlic general intelligence test or the Bennett AA general mechanical test.

The U.S. Supreme Court concluded in the *Griggs* case that such devices have a disparate impact on blacks and could not be justified by business necessity in this case.[49] (Under the business necessity rule, an employer can use a selection device that produces a disparate impact on the basis of race or sex only if the employer can demonstrate that the test is necessary for the business's efficient operation. In the case of a test, an employer must demonstrate validity under the standards accepted by social scientists in the field of testing.) Because employers such as Duke Power have been unable to construct the evidence of test validity required under this standard, they no longer routinely use general intelligence tests to select employees.[50] One might have expected law and economics scholars to applaud this result, as it encourages employers to choose efficient, job-related selection devices rather than rely on presumptions about correlations between test scores and job performance. Instead, this line of cases has been roundly criticized as making it too expensive for employers to use testing and educational requirements that can withstand judicial scrutiny.

Richard Epstein has led the charge against requiring validation of such tests, claiming that testing serves a valuable purpose. His source for this claim is the industry that creates and promotes these tests:

Notwithstanding their embattled status under Title VII, there is a widespread belief on the part of those who design and use general employment tests that these provide accurate and essential predictions of job success for individual workers and should therefore be regarded as an important, indeed an indispensable, aid in hiring and promotion decisions.[51]

Epstein's reasoning is circular. He insists that we should permit educational and testing requirements to give young people an incentive to obtain more education. "[B]y reducing the returns on education, it removes one of the incentives that young people have to expend money, time, and effort on acquiring an education."[52] But we could also caution young people from thinking that more education always leads to more employment opportunities. They may want to consider other reasons for seeking higher education, such as the intrinsic satisfaction gained or the differing types of jobs that may become available. Young people who choose to pursue a doctoral degree in the humanities must recognize that they might earn more money simply by completing an inexpensive certificate program in the health care field, yet presumably they make their choice for its intrinsic value. Carried to its logical conclusion, however, Epstein's argument would permit employers to bar from low-level employment anyone who could not obtain high test scores or a college diploma, regardless of his or her aptitude for that particular job. But many employers would be quite mistaken in assuming that law professors, for example, who score well on general intelligence tests would be competent to fulfill the kind of mechanical position that was at stake in *Griggs*.

Another employment device that often harms the employment opportunities of blacks is word-of-mouth recruiting. The American labor force is heavily segregated along racial lines.

Because of segregation in friendship and housing patterns, word-of-mouth recruiting helps perpetuate those segregated patterns at the workplace. As the Fifth Circuit concluded in 1973, word-of-mouth recruiting "operates as a 'built-in-head-wind' to blacks" at a workforce in which only 7.2 percent of the employees are black.[53] Similarly, a 1994 University of Minnesota study of poor youths in Boston found that the blacks in the sample had more schooling but lower wages than the whites did, because the whites had better employment contacts. "Whites who found jobs through relatives earned 38 percent more than the blacks who did. But for those who got jobs without contacts, the white-black earning gap was only 5 percent."[54] Word-of-mouth recruiting, therefore, affects both employability and wages.

Word-of-mouth recruiting has been upheld as "efficient" even when the evidence demonstrates that it would have been equally efficient to notify the state unemployment service of a job opening. Then, however, the applicants would have been disproportionately black, given the disproportionately high rate of unemployment in the black community. Unemployment by a particular racial group is easily perpetuated if word-of-mouth recruiting rather than notification of the state unemployment office is the primary method of recruitment for entry-level jobs. This is an example of unconscious racism that also serves as a self-perpetuating form of discrimination. An employer may choose to pursue an application process that minimizes its costs, but will it choose to notify the state unemployment office, or will it encourage its employees to tell their friends and relatives about the job openings?

Although both mechanisms are cheap and thus efficient, the first process usually results in large numbers of minority applicants, and the second usually does not (that is, not in an already segregated workplace). Hence as early as 1968, Professor Alfred Blumrosen, who also worked for the Equal Employment Opportunity Commission (EEOC), suggested that "a requirement outside of the South that all employers utilize the employment service with respect to all jobs will benefit Negro job seekers to a proportionally greater extent than white, and should be imposed."[55] A search for efficiency, combined with either conscious or unconscious racism, may result in the choice of word-of-mouth recruitment. The Seventh Circuit ratified word-of-mouth recruitment as consistent with the principles of efficiency and thereby presumed that it is also consistent with the principle of nondiscrimination. The EEOC's argument in these cases that state employment services were not, but should have been, used for employment advertising was ignored. There is no reason to equate efficiency with nondiscrimination. Several efficient sources for employees exist. Why, then, was this particular device chosen?

When word-of-mouth recruitment results in few black applicants, the Seventh Circuit blames the black applicants rather than the employer's recruitment practices. Thus, in *EEOC v. Chicago Miniature Lamp Work*,[56] the Seventh Circuit held against the black plaintiffs (reversing the trial court's decision) in a case in which the plaintiffs had complained of discrimination in recruitment. The Seventh Circuit found that because the factory was in a Hispanic and Asian part of Chicago, it was unrealistic to expect blacks to want to work there. It blamed the low application rates for blacks on their lack of interest in such jobs rather than on any affirmative actions by the employer. In the court's words: "[The company] is not liable when it passively relies on the natural flow of applicants for its entry-level positions."

Eight years later, in *EEOC v. Consolidated Service Systems*, the *Miniature* holding was transformed into the conclusion that word-of-mouth recruitment is inherently "efficient" and "cheap."[57] This time, the company was located in the majority-black city of Chicago. Reliance on word-of-mouth recruiting, however, resulted in a small African American applicant pool. Despite the apparent irrationality of the applicant pool, Judge Posner, writing for the Seventh Circuit, was heavily persuaded by the efficiency of Consolidated's hiring practices. No fewer than four times, Posner repeated that Consolidated picked the cheapest and most efficient method of hiring, that is, word-of-mouth recruitment. As he stated, "[I]t is clear[,] as we have been at pains to emphasize, [that it is] the cheapest and most efficient method of recruitment, notwithstanding its discriminatory impact." Posner's nonempirical assertion about efficiency entirely overlooked the efficiency of notifying the state unemployment office of job openings.

Posner's unsupported assertions also recently appeared again in a dissenting opinion by Seventh Circuit Judge Daniel Manion, another proponent of conservative economic principles. This case also reflected serious problems with an employer's recruitment and hiring process, with the result that absolutely no blacks were hired in a six-year period, even though the plant was located in a predominantly black neighborhood. Manion chose to ignore the overwhelming statistics in the case, concluding that "English-speaking job seekers may not want to work in an environment of predominantly foreign languages."[58] As in the *Chicago Miniature Lamp Works* case, he concluded that the lack of interest by blacks in the area was more likely to explain the low rate of black employment than was an act of discrimination by the employer, O&G Spring & Wire Forms.

The only evidence confirming the interest of blacks in such employment contradicts Manion's assertion. A complaint of discrimination filed with the EEOC resulted in a dramatic increase in applications by African Americans at the company.[59] Did African Americans suddenly become interested in working alongside non-English-speaking employees? As with the affirmative action cases, Judge Manion made assumptions about blacks that one would not make about whites. This case reflected an employment setting in which Polish Americans and Spanish-speaking Americans worked side by side. Although these two groups of whites did not have a common language, they appeared to be comfortable with each other in the workplace. Judge Manion assumed, however, that African Americans, who spoke yet a different language, would not be comfortable working alongside these two groups.

Manion also overlooked the arguments available in this case concerning economic rationality. Unlike the *Consolidated Services* case, O&G was located in the heart of a predominantly black neighborhood. It was therefore economically rational for blacks to seek employment there. Accordingly, since Manion could not claim economic rationality, he invented national origin or language animus on the part of African Americans, but with no testimony on record to support it. It was far easier to blame unemployed blacks for their low employment record than to blame O&G's management.

Manion's theme strongly reflects the values of efficiency and objectivity found in law and economics. To bolster his efficiency argument, he quoted Judge Posner's opinion in *Consolidated Service*: "It would be a bitter irony if the federal agency dedicated to enforcing the antidiscrimination laws succeeded in using those laws to kick these people off the ladder by compelling them to institute costly systems of hiring."[60] According to this "logic," word-of-mouth recruiting should be tolerated because it is purportedly the cheapest method, even if it knowingly results in a loss of employment opportunities for African Americans.

Applying the principle of objectivity, Manion contended that there was no way to argue why one subgroup deserves preferential treatment over another subgroup. "By not taking the language factor into consideration the EEOC has in effect put a quota on one vulnerable group at the expense of another." But the "language factor" was Judge Manion's invention, because the evidence showed that it did not deter the employment of two groups of whites at that workplace.

The clever move in Judge Manion's opinion was to twist a requirement for equal treatment—giving blacks and others an equal opportunity to hear about openings and be hired at O&G—into a "quota" that apparently pitted "one vulnerable group" against another. Affirmative action is considered inefficient because it reflects non-merit-based preferences for blacks, but word-of-mouth recruitment for nonblacks is considered permissible because it is efficient, even though it grants non-merit-based preferences to nonblacks. The measure of efficiency is the extent of black employment. When black employment rises, we must attribute it to "quota madness" rather than the removal of barriers toward advancement.[61] But when white employment declines, we must attribute it to affirmative action. Black employment thus is inefficient, whereas white employment is efficient.

### The Canadian Experience

The United States' evocation of the merit principle is not inevitable. Canada, for example, seems to have escaped many of the problems surrounding the hiring and educational practices in the United States. Testing for education or employment is not as widespread in Canada as it is in the United States. Affirmative action is constitutionally protected for members of historically disadvantaged groups. Not only has the affirmative action principle been extended to women and racial minorities, but claims by gays and lesbians have also been recognized under this principle. Canadian universities are generally public institutions and do not share the money-conscious perspective of elite American private universities. A formal bar exam does not serve as a barrier to admission to the Canadian bar; instead, a more practice-oriented process is used to determine who is qualified to practice law.

Unlike American jurisprudence on equality issues, Canadian jurisprudence is comparative in nature. The experience of other countries as well as international human rights conventions influence the decisions rendered by Canadian judges. Although U.S. precedent is often cited, Canadian courts often refuse to follow it because it is out of step with the jurisprudence of other Western nations. Thus, the legal perspective plus substantive conclusions by Canadian judges differ markedly from those of U.S. judges, even though the two countries have similar histories and geographies.

The source of the substantive differences between Canadian and American equality jurisprudence can be found in their respective constitutions. The Fourteenth Amendment to the U.S. Constitution states that "all persons" are entitled to "equal protection under the law." This approach, which is usually described as "formal equality," permits judges to treat claims of discrimination brought by white men in the same way as they do claims of discrimination brought by African-American women. In addition, this approach subjects affirmative action measures on behalf of women or racial minorities to discrimination claims by white men. And as we have seen, judges who subscribe to extreme laissez-faire principles are very sympathetic to these reverse discrimination claims.

Reverse discrimination claims are generally not recognized in Canadian jurisprudence. The right to equal treatment is protected under Section 15 of the Canadian Charter of Rights and Freedoms. Part 1 of Section 15 is similar to the Fourteenth Amendment of the U.S. Constitution. It provides for the individual right to equal treatment under the law. Canadian courts, however, have interpreted this rule differently than have U.S. courts. Proof of discrimination may come through proof of discriminatory purpose (as in the United States) or through proof of discriminatory effect (unlike the United States). Thus, in the previous example involving a claim of discrimination by Asian Americans by the use of the alumni preference rule, a Canadian court would consider those plaintiffs to have invoked a prima facie case of racial discrimination based solely on the effect of the rule.

Canadian courts, however, have imposed an additional requirement on a discrimination claim that is not found in the United States. Plaintiffs who allege discrimination must demonstrate that their claim of discrimination is based on an enumerated or analogous ground to a disadvantaged group. Enumerated grounds include race, national or ethnic origin, color, religion, sex, age, or mental or physical disability—which are specified directly in Part 1 of Section 15. Analogous grounds are additional characteristics that the courts have found similarly stem from disadvantage and therefore should be protected from discrimination. Marital status, sexual orientation, citizenship, and being adoptive parents or adoptive children have been found to constitute analogous grounds. Thus, not all "persons" can bring claims of discrimination; they must be able to demonstrate a history of disadvantaged treatment.

If a Canadian plaintiff establishes a prima facie case of discrimination, the burden of proof shifts to the government or other party upholding the law. Two defenses are recognized under Canadian law. The government can argue that the challenged rule implements an affirmative action program permitted under Part 2 of Section 15 or that the violation of the equality provisions is reasonably and demonstrably justified in a free and democratic society as permitted under Section 1 of the Charter.

Section 15, Part 2, was included in the Charter in order to save applicable affirmative action programs from a finding of constitutional invalidity. Part 2 operates to excuse the violation of Section 15, Part 1, if the persons in favor of whom the distinction is made are disadvantaged and the object of the discrimination is the amelioration of that disadvantage. Part 2 states that Part 1 "does not preclude any law, program or activity that has as its object the amelioration of conditions of disadvantaged individuals or groups including those that are disadvantaged because of race, national or ethnic origin, color, religion, sex, age or mental or physical disability." Canadian courts have developed three principles to assist in the application of Section 15, Part 2: (1) There must be a rational connection between the preferential treatment and the disadvantage; (2) there must be a real nexus between the object of the program as declared by the government and its form and implementation; and (3) the burden of proof under this part rests on the party seeking to invoke this part to demonstrate its application.[62]

The application of these three principles reflects a compromise on affirmative action. It was not intended to save from scrutiny all legislation intended to have an ameliorative effect. Instead, it was included to silence the debate that rages in the United States and elsewhere concerning the legitimacy of affirmative action while requiring that affirmative action programs pass muster only when they are reasonably effective and appropriately tailored programs.

In the Canadian courts, nearly all the cases challenging affirmative action programs have been unsuccessful. And unlike the United States, most of the cases have not involved race-based affirmative action. Gender and disability cases have also played a prominent role in the development of this line of cases. In those cases that look most like the United States' reverse discrimination cases—claims brought by able-bodied white men— the courts have been resoundingly unsympathetic to the plaintiff.[63] Those cases that given the courts pause have been ones in which both the plaintiff and the intended beneficiary class under the affirmative action plan were members of a disadvantaged group. In such cases, the courts have tried to wrestle with what the content of an affirmative action program would be that benefits as many disadvantaged groups as possible.

A recent Ontario case, *Schafer v. Attorney General*,[64] reflects a tension between two disadvantaged groups as well as a sophisticated analysis of the tension between Parts 1 and 2 of Section 15. The opinion reflects an attempt to create a social policy that benefits as much of society as possible while not assuming that government intervention itself is objectionable.

The plaintiffs challenged Canada's Unemployment Insurance Act with respect to its rules regarding maternity and child care benefits. The plaintiffs were adoptive parents who were given less paid leave under the Unemployment Insurance Act than were similarly situated biological parents. The biological parents received five additional weeks of child care benefits that were not made available to parents who adopted their children when they were under the age of six months. Biological parents could receive up to twenty-five weeks of maternity and child care benefits, compared with ten weeks for adoptive parents.

The case reflected a tension between Parts 1 and 2 of Section 15 of the Canadian Charter because the government defended the program by arguing that the maternity and child care benefits rule had been enacted to ameliorate the conditions of women who are disadvantaged, that is, unable to work, because of their sex or because of their physical disability due to pregnancy and childbirth. Being aware of the requirement that a valid program under Part 2 must be reasonably related to its ameliorative purposes, the government further argued that the rule was effective in achieving its objective and that there was a direct relationship between the cause of the disadvantage and the form of the ameliorative action. Since women who give birth face a period of physical disability, the government contended that adoptive parents are not similarly situated in needing the ameliorative treatment.

The first part of the analysis required the court to determine when plaintiffs had a cognizable claim of discrimination under Part 1 of Section 15. To have a proper claim under Part 1, the plaintiffs needed to establish that they had a claim of discrimination on the basis of an enumerated or analogous ground. Because adoptive parents and children are not specifically enumerated in Part 1 of Section 15, they had to pursue the analogous ground arguments.

To support the claim that they were a group deserving antidiscrimination protection under Part 1 of Section 15, the plaintiffs referred to international conventions as well as the practice in other countries. Both the Universal Declaration of Human Rights and the Convention on the Rights of the Child state that special measures of protection and assistance should be taken on behalf of all children, without discrimination on the basis of parentage. In addition, these conventions recognize the need to provide paid leave to mothers following the birth or adoption of a child. Surveying the practices of other Western countries, the court also noted that most of them provide for paid maternity leave consistent with the various international conventions. The United States, however, the court noted, does not provide for federally mandated paid maternity leave and has also not endorsed the International Labor Organization's Maternity Protection Convention. Based on this comparative examination, the Canadian court concluded that adoptive parents and their children should be protected from discrimination under Part 1 of Section 15 because their need to be protected from discrimination has been widely recognized in the Western world.

Having found that the plaintiffs did establish a prima facie case of discrimination, the court had to determine whether such discrimination could be justified under Part 2 of Section 15 (the affirmative action exception) or under Section 1 (the exception for rules that are reasonably and demonstrably justified in a free and democratic society). Turning first to the affirmative action justification, the Ontario court rejected the argument that there was a close nexus between the program and the cause of the disadvantage, because the leave rule provided greater benefits than are necessary in the great majority of cases to respond to the physical disability of pregnancy. In other words, the program provided direct financial support during family formation, which would be as useful to biological parents as to adoptive parents. The fact that the program had an ameliorative objective did not save it under Part 2 of Section 15 because the court found that the alleged benefit was only a collateral effect of the program. The primary benefit was providing financial support during family formation.

The analysis of Part 2 was not the end of the inquiry under Canadian constitutional law. The government also had the opportunity to defend the program as reasonably and demonstrably justified in a free and democratic society. Here, the analysis focused on the good to society of the program rather than on the discrete harm to the plaintiffs. At this point, both the government and the plaintiffs agreed that the objectives of the program were substantial—that the child, family, and society benefited from programs that facilitated family formation. The government argued that cost considerations should permit it to limit to biological families the scope of policies designed to facilitate family formation. But the court rejected this argument, stating that cost factors should not be given much weight under Section 1. In the court's words: "If the government is able to get away with violating a constitutionally protected right because of cost consequences, of what use is the Charter?" Rather than start from the presumption of laissez-faire economics, the Canadian court started from the presumption that government intervention is appropriate and, in some cases, should be mandated. The result of this particular legal challenge was to require the government to extend its unemployment insurance benefits to adoptive parents. Rather than strike down an ameliorative program for biological mothers as being inconsistent with affirmative action principles, it extended the ameliorative program to another disadvantaged class. It sought to maximize the benefits of family support programs for all of society while also guarding against unnecessary discrimination.

The Canadian experience shows that state intervention need not exclusively serve the interests of the propertied class. State intervention can instead try to overturn a history of discrimination against disadvantaged classes in society. Such intervention is accepted not simply because it assists underprivileged members of society but because it serves the interests of all of society for people to achieve their human potential.

By examining diverse areas of the law such as alumni preference in admission to educational institutions and word-of-mouth recruitment in employment settings, we can uncover values that otherwise might remain hidden. Alumni preferences for white children and word-of-mouth recruiting for white employees are practices that help perpetuate a class advantage for a subgroup of whites in our society. Despite the inefficiency of disrupting the merit principle by limiting the applicant pool or creating a two-tiered definition of merit, these practices are upheld as praiseworthy. When blacks try to change the rules so that they, too, can gain access to education or employment, they are told by whites that they are perpetuating stereotypes and stigma through affirmative action or "quota madness." It is time for whites to examine their own sources of privileged affirmative action—from private schools to safe neighborhoods to good nutrition—and ask whether their success is really based solely on "merit." For law to be truly color blind, we must locate and describe white privilege, not simply criticize modest attempts by blacks to attempt to even the score.

# 3

# DISABILITY DISCRIMINATION

*Wall Street Journal* columnist James Bovard ridiculed the Americans with Disabilities Act (ADA) by suggesting that claustrophobia and cocaine addiction are covered disabilities, invoking reasonable accommodation protection.[1] He tells a story of a motorist attempting to use claustrophobia as a defense for a seatbelt violation but fails to mention that the motorist's case was dismissed and brought strong negative commentary from the court.[2] Similarly, Bovard reports that a high school guidance counselor used the ADA to challenge his cocaine-related discharge, neglecting to mention that the state court action[3] did not (and could not) include an ADA claim, because the ADA excludes current users of illegal drugs from statutory coverage. *Wall Street Journal* reporter Stephanie Mehta made the unfounded accusation that "the cost of [ADA] compliance has probably affected many small business profit margins,"[4] ignoring the fact that most private employers were already subject to similar standards under state disability discrimination law long before the ADA was passed. A *San Francisco Chronicle* editorial stated that the term *disability* as used under the ADA is "a highly questionable definition that fails to differentiate between people in wheelchairs and junkies,"[5] plainly ignoring the statutory definition of a person with a disability.

Law and economics scholar Richard Epstein argued that people with disabilities would benefit more from governmental noninterference than from disability discrimination laws, stating, "Like everyone else, the disabled should be allowed to sell their labor at whatever price, and on whatever terms, they see fit."[6] Mandatory affirmative action or reasonable accommodation requirements, he says, are ineffective and unjustifiable tools. He describes the supporters of such remedial devices as " antilibertarian, antiutilitarian, and antimarket in their orientation."[7]

Why this campaign of lies and distortions? Why this onslaught against the ADA by some proponents of law and economics? The simple answer is that vigorous enforcement of disability discrimination law stands in opposition to laissez-faire economics. Hence, the *Wall Street Journal* enlists any possible tactic to undermine the public's confidence in the ADA. Employing more rational arguments, the supporters of a law and economics perspective attempt to demonstrate that antidiscrimination law is inefficient and unprincipled.

Resistance to state-sanctioned remedial action on behalf of people with disabilities—and, in essence, all members of historically disadvantaged groups in the United States—is partly a reflection of a laissez-faire economic perspective. According to free-market principles, the state should not require that the pri-

vate sector use preferential programs to improve the employability of members of disadvantaged groups because there is no
objective way to determine who is historically disadvantaged
and because state intervention in private markets is an inefficient remedy for any social problem.

As applied to the law of disability discrimination, this perspective yields two arguments. First, it contends that the state
should not define one subgroup—people with disabilities—as
deserving special, statutory protection. Second, it asserts that
the state should not mandate reasonable accommodations for
people with disabilities because such programs constitute preferential measures.

The first argument is made possible because of a distinctive
feature of disability discrimination law. Rather than protecting
any person who can claim discrimination (including reverse discrimination) on the basis of disability, the ADA protects only
those persons who qualify as "person[s] with a disability." There
are no reverse discrimination claims under the ADA; the statute
recognizes claims of discriminatory treatment only by persons
with disabilities. This feature is distinctive because it is not
shared by Title VII of the Civil Rights Act of 1964. Under Title
VII, anyone can file a claim of discrimination on the basis of
race, sex, national origin, or religion because each person has a
race, sex, national origin, and religion. One does not have to be
a woman or racial minority to bring a claim of discrimination;
reverse discrimination claims are cognizable by white men. The
Title VII approach is more consistent with laissez-faire principles than is the ADA approach because it does not define a subgroup as deserving special statutory protection. Laissez-faire
proponents thus question the legitimacy of the state's determining that a particular subgroup—people with disabilities—

deserve statutory protection that is not available to others in society.

The second argument is made possible because reasonable accommodations are really a type of affirmative action. Proponents of disability discrimination law have tried to hide this fact by arguing that reasonable accommodation does not constitute "affirmative action." But in fact, some forms of reasonable accommodation, such as job restructuring or job reassignment, can be considered a type of affirmative action. (Hence, law and economics proponents are correct to consider reasonable accommodation to be a type of affirmative action.) The backlash against these and other forms of reasonable accommodation can theoretically be tied to the backlash against race- and sex-based affirmative action—an attempt to use laissez-faire economic arguments to challenge the appropriateness of mandated preferential measures for any subgroup in society. When seen in this light, the story of how the courts, society, and the media have responded to the law of disability discrimination in the United States further illuminates the role of hypercapitalism in attacking affirmative action principles.

In the United States, hostility toward affirmative action has grown greatly in the last decade, with legal decisions following this political trend. In the last decade, the U.S. Supreme Court has found in favor of white claimants in several recent leading cases.[8] Racism—or the denial of its magnitude—is the typical liberal explanation for this trend. Accordingly, Justice Thurgood Marshall chastised the majority in a reverse discrimination case for failing to acknowledge the relevance of the legacy of discrimination in Richmond, Virginia, the former capital of the Confederacy: "As much as any municipality in the United States, Richmond knows what racial discrimination is; a century of decisions by this and other federal courts have richly documented the city's disgraceful history of public and private racial discrimination."[9] Ignoring this history, the Supreme Court ruled that the city of Richmond could not institute a policy that gave preference to contractors who promised to utilize minority subcontractors when working for the city.

Although the denial of racism is certainly a factor in the backlash to affirmative action, it is not the only important explanation. Affirmative action and laissez-faire economics stand in tension with each other. Free-market principles conflict with the imposition of broad-based remedial programs to assist members of specified, historically disadvantaged groups. As applied to the Americans with Disabilities Act, these principles call for resistance to reasonable accommodation measures and an unwillingness to define a subgroup in society as deserving special statutory protection.

The varying commitment of the United States, Great Britain, Canada, and Australia to a pure laissez-faire model can also help us understand the differences in their support of the law of disability discrimination. The United States and Great Britain are relatively more laissez-faire (in recent times) than are Canada and Australia. The United States has never had a strong labor party, has no system of nationalized health insurance, and has a relatively weak labor union movement. Great Britain's Labour Party only recently emerged from twenty years of disfavor, and the labor union movement is still suffering from a sharp decline. Great Britain does have nationalized health insurance, but that fact can be tied to the Labour Party's earlier power rather than its current strength in British politics. In recent years, labor parties in Canada and Australia have won major elections at the federal or regional level. The New Democratic Party was recently in power in Ontario, Canada, and the Liberal government is in power at the federal level. Australia's Labour Party recently ended an extended period of party dominance at the federal level. Like Great Britain, Canada and Australia have nationalized health insurance. Canada also has a small military and did not engage in the cold war. It has far less hostile relations with the emerging socialist and communist regimes of other countries than does the United States or Great Britain. The two countries with the strongest commitment to laissez-faire economics—United States and Great Britain—are the most resistant to what they perceive to be affirmative action or special treatment (including reasonable accommodation for people with disabilities).

Admittedly, the economic distinctions among these four countries are small. Nonetheless, many Americans misunderstand the depth of the differences in philosophy and economics between the United States and its neighbor, Canada. As we will see, the differences between American and Canadian disability jurisprudence are stark.

This inquiry also gives us added insight into the connection between law and politics. In the United States, the imposition of reasonable accommodation requirements under disability discrimination law has had little effect on the scope of protection for people with disabilities. Legal decisions imbued in laissez-faire economics have badly warped the underlying structure of disability discrimination law. For example, although reasonable accommodation is required under U.S. law and only permitted under Canadian law, the courts have more vigorously enforced a reasonable accommodation requirement in Canada than in the United States.

Of course, language is not entirely meaningless. U.S. courts have had to (reluctantly) impose some reasonable accommodation requirements and have not been able to permit reverse discrimination suits, since able-bodied persons have no standing to bring suit. Nonetheless, the interpretation of these statutes is more a reflection of the politics of economics than of statutory language.

## Reasonable Accommodation as Affirmative Action

Consider the following six related terms:

- Nondiscrimination
- Reasonable accommodation
- Positive action
- Preferential treatment
- Affirmative action
- Reverse discrimination

These are their conventional definitions:

*Nondiscrimination* reflects the removal of blatant stereotypes and prejudices so that people can be treated based on their merit.

*Reasonable accommodation* reflects the removal of barriers that society has created so that qualified persons can demonstrate their merit.

*Preferential treatment, positive action,* and *affirmative action* reflect the redefinition of merit to enable the traits and abilities of members of historically disadvantaged groups to be given greater value.

*Reverse discrimination* reflects the awarding of an automatic advantage to a member of a historically disadvantaged group so that this person can have a greater opportunity of being selected for a position.

These terms describe programs designed to improve the employability of historically disadvantaged groups in our society. As we move across these categories, we move from general legal and social acceptance to legal and social disapproval. In particular, whether a program is defined as reasonable accommodation or affirmative action is often considered to signal its acceptability or legality. For example, as (British) Professor Brian Doyle stated: "The idea of reasonable accommodation has often been misunderstood and mistaken as a form of preferential treatment or positive action. . . . The erroneous association of reasonable accommodation with forms of preferential treatment, however, will be a difficult perception to erase in the minds of many employers."[10] Although Doyle's statement may be politically expedient (in justifying reasonable accommodation rules at the time of an affirmative action backlash), it is technically incorrect. Affirmative action should also be considered to be a type of reasonable accommodation.

An example demonstrates the elusiveness and political significance of these categories. In *Johnson v. Transportation Agency*,[11] the Supreme Court considered the constitutionality of a promotion that was awarded in accordance with an affirmative action plan. Both Diane Joyce and Paul Johnson applied for a promotion from a road maintenance worker to a road dispatcher. Until 1975, Joyce had worked in the traditionally female job classification of account clerk. When she applied for a promotion in 1974 to a road dispatcher position, she was denied it because she had not served in the traditionally male job classification of road maintenance worker. The definition of merit—experience as a road maintenance worker—precluded her from occupational advancement. In 1975 Joyce then transferred from a senior account clerk position to a road maintenance worker in order to qualify for the dispatcher position. She was the first woman to fill the road maintenance position. While serving in this position, she was initially not issued the work clothes that were routinely issued to men, and she was described as a "rebel-rousing skirt-wearing person." After serving in the road maintenance position for four years, Joyce applied for a promotion to road dispatcher. A major factor in the selection process was an interview, conducted by three supervisors, two of whom had been involved in the discriminatory incidents previously mentioned. Joyce received a score of 73 on the interview. Paul Johnson, a man with less road maintenance experience, received a score of 75 on the interview and was recommended for the promotion. When Joyce learned that Johnson had been recommended for the promotion, she contacted the affirmative action officer. Based on the affirmative action officer's intervention, Joyce was promoted to the position.

Johnson then challenged Joyce's promotion as violating his rights under Title VII of the Civil Rights Act of 1964. A divided Supreme Court ruled that the promotion did not violate Title VII. Although a majority of the Court concluded that the county had taken into account Joyce's sex in determining who should be awarded the promotion, it concluded that this explicit use of sex was appropriate because it followed a "moderate, flexible, case-by-case approach to effecting a gradual improvement in the representation of minorities and women in the Agency's work force." In its statement of the facts, the Court emphasized the evidence that Joyce had been a direct victim of sex discrimination while serving as a road maintenance worker. One could therefore view the intervention by the affirmative action officer as simply ridding the promotion process of explicit sex-based discrimination.

Justice Sandra Day O'Connor's concurrence described the selection process as one in which Joyce was given a "plus" because of her sex but argued that Joyce was not "automatically and blindly" promoted because of her sex. O'Connor therefore considered the application of the affirmative action plan in this instance to be an example of preferential treatment rather than reverse discrimination. In a biting dissent, Justice Antonin Scalia, joined by Justices William Rehnquist and Byron White, complained that

> a statute designed to establish a color-blind and gender-blind workplace has thus been converted into a powerful engine of racism and sexism, not merely *permitting* intentional race- and sex-based discrimination, but often making it, through operation of the legal system, practically compelled. . . . [T]he only losers in the process are the Johnsons of the country, for whom Title VII has been not merely repealed but actually inverted.

For the dissenters, this case was a classic example of reverse discrimination, in which a male blue-collar worker was the victim of a non-merit-based decision.

These opinions reflect the numerous ways in which a program designed to improve the employability of women and minorities can be described as a case of nondiscrimination, preferential treatment, affirmative action, or reverse discrimination, depending on one's legal, economic, and political perspective. The categories are arguably interchangeable, offering different ways for the state to require that private employers take steps to improve the employability of historically disadvantaged groups.

For example, a typical explanation is that rather than preferential treatment, people with disabilities often need accommodations that remove barriers at the workplace: "Reasonable accommodation involves the making of modifications or adjustments to the employment process and to the workplace environment so as to ensure that disabled persons are not discriminated against, but may enjoy equal opportunities with others."[12] Thus, if a workplace has five steps leading to the entrance, those steps become a barrier to employment for a person who uses a wheelchair. A reasonable accommodation would be removing the barrier (and probably replacing it with a ramp). But it would not result in the disabled person's being given a "plus" so that he or she might be hired over an equally qualified, nondisabled employee, which is the common understanding of affirmative action.

Affirmative action on the basis of race or gender, however, can also be considered within the "remove the barrier" metaphor. For example, some cities have modified their firefighter selection examinations in order to give women or minorities greater opportunities to obtain employment;[13] school districts have modified their workplace rules in order to eliminate a barrier to minorities retaining their jobs during a layoff;[14] and counties, as in the *Johnson* case, have disregarded subjective criteria in order to enhance women's employment opportunities. Disability accommodations may often require the removal of physical barriers, but the operational practice under race and sex discrimination law is analogous—modifying rules to create equal opportunity when those rules are not necessary to the job. In fact, the defenses available to employers in reasonable accommodation cases are fundamentally similar to the defenses available to employers under the business necessity doctrine developed by the U.S. courts for disproportionate impact cases in *Griggs v. Duke Power*[15] and codified by the U.S. Congress in the 1991 Civil Rights Act.[16] According to these theories, those rules that operate as barriers to employment must be modified if they cannot be justified by business necessity. The removal of these barriers can be described as affirmative action or reasonable accommodation.

By considering reasonable accommodation to be a type of affirmative action, we can better assess the sources of the legal and political resistance to affirmative action when a stereotypical "quota" system is not at issue. (I use the term *stereotypical* because I believe that race- and gender-based affirmative action is often misunderstood by the public. Since *Regents of the University of California v. Bakke*[17] was decided, quotas have been disfavored and rarely used. Yet when I ask my students to define "affirmative action," "quotas" is usually their first response.) Courts sometimes reject claims for reasonable accommodation as inappropriate requests for "affirmative action." Conservative theorists from the field of law and economics often do not distinguish between reasonable accommodation and affirmative action when arguing that civil rights law should be repealed; liberal theorists also have to be aware of the connection between these principles.

Nonetheless, the equation of reasonable accommodation with affirmative action is particularly controversial because reasonable accommodation is a term usually applied only to disability cases. In the United States, however, affirmative action is a term usually applied only to race and gender cases. This pattern does not exist in Canada. Instead, Canada developed the principle of reasonable accommodation for religion, age, and pregnancy discrimination cases nearly a decade before this concept was applied to disability cases. The concept of reasonable accommodation also exists in American law for religious discrimination cases, but the definition of reasonable accommodation is quite narrow, in part because of our antiestablishment clause.[18] An antiestablishment clause does not exist in the Canadian constitution.

To understand the concept of affirmative action in the legal traditions of different countries, it is important to recognize that this term reflects a particular country's determination of who has faced historical discrimination. In the United States, for example, we usually think of racial discrimination when we discuss affirmative action. In Canada, by contrast, affirmative action discussions often focus on gender equality issues or the historical situation of Native Canadians. Race discrimination is not the primary metaphor. Great Britain does not have a tradition of affirmative action (or as the British call it, *positive action*) pertaining to race or gender. As we will see in chapter 4, however, after World War II, Great Britain enacted an affirmative quota system for hiring people with disabilities. Thus it is too simplistic to say that a country that does not adopt extreme laissez-faire economic views accepts affirmative action for all potentially disadvantaged groups in its society. The country's attitude toward the appropriateness of affirmative action is tempered by its historical understanding of which groups in society have faced historical discrimination.

### United States Case Law

#### INTRODUCTION

Disability discrimination law is a new area of civil rights protection in the United States. The movement for disability rights in the United States has been influenced by the movements for civil rights on the basis of race and sex, but its model of protection is quite different: it tolerates preferential treatment exclusively for members of a historically disadvantaged class.

Preferential treatment for historically disadvantaged groups is legally disfavored under race and sex antidiscrimination law in the United States, but "reverse discrimination" claims have virtually overtaken race and gender antidiscrimination law. Nearly all the cases on discrimination issues decided by the U.S. Supreme Court in the last several terms have been reverse discrimination cases. In case after case, the Supreme Court found for the white plaintiff. By contrast, most of the claims brought by women and minorities were unsuccessful.

Such developments made me snidely inquire whether we should object to a Republican Congress's trying to repeal antidiscrimination law, since in recent years, it rarely has served the interests of women or minorities.[19] Ironically, Epstein would agree with me that affirmative action might flourish more easily in the absence of antidiscrimination law, since reverse discrimination lawsuits would no longer be recognized: "Were discrimination allowed as a matter of course, the greatest victory for the civil rights movement would be to see its own position prevail in an atmosphere wholly free from any threat of government coercion."[20] Epstein does not argue that affirmative action itself is a bad idea; rather, he believes that government should not impose affirmative action on the private sector.

Such preferential treatment is often called *reverse discrimination*. Title VII of the Civil Rights Act of 1964 says that it is unlawful for an employer to discriminate against an "individual" because of such individual's race, color, religion, sex, or national origin. Because we each have a "race" or "sex," we are covered by the statute, regardless of whether we are a historically disadvantaged race or sex. Similarly, the Fourteenth Amendment to the U.S. Constitution states that no state shall "deny to any person within its jurisdiction the equal protection of the laws." Because we each are "persons," we are covered by the Constitution regardless of our particular race or sex. Race and sex antidiscrimination law is therefore an "antidifferentiation" approach rather than an "antisubordination" approach.[21] As an antidifferentiation approach, it seeks to eliminate all distinctions on the basis of race and sex rather than to respond to the needs of historically disadvantaged groups.

By contrast, disability discrimination law requires preferential treatment through reasonable accommodation. The ADA defines a "qualified individual with a disability" who is entitled to nondiscrimination protection to include "an individual with a disability who, with, or without reasonable accommodation can perform the essential functions of the employment position that such individual holds or desires." It does not try to require only neutral nondiscrimination. It is embedded in an antisubordination rather than an antidifferentiation approach. It seeks to improve the employability of a historically disadvantaged group—people with disabilities—rather than to eliminate all disability distinctions from society.

The class of people protected under race and sex antidiscrimination law and disability discrimination law is also quite different. Title VII does not limit coverage to members of a historically disadvantaged group. Any *individual* can bring a lawsuit under race and sex antidiscrimination law. In an early case, the Supreme Court decided that this individual could be a white man who was claiming "reverse" discrimination.[22] Thus, nearly any individual who has an employment relationship with a covered employer can bring suit under race and sex antidiscrimination law.

Disability discrimination law, however, allows only those individuals who are "qualified individuals with disabilities" to file a claim of discrimination. A qualified individual with a disability is an "individual with a disability who satisfies the requisite skill, experience, education and other job-related requirements of the employment position such individual holds or desires, and who, with or without reasonable accommodation, can perform the essential functions of the job." To be considered disabled, a person typically must demonstrate that he or she has an impairment that substantially limits a major life activity. The term *disability* means (1) a physical or mental impairment that substantially limits one or more of an individual's major life activities or (2) a record of such an impairment or (3) being regarded as having such an impairment. Claims of discrimination are therefore available only to members of a historically disadvantaged group; there is no such thing as a "reverse" discrimination disability claim.

Although disability discrimination law explicitly incorporates an antisubordination approach, and race and sex discrimination law formally favor an antidifferentiation approach, both areas of American law favor the antidifferentiation approach in practice. Courts in the United States have undermined the preferential treatment principles underlying disability discrimination law, despite the clear statutory language to the contrary. They also have narrowed the category of potential claimants entitled to statutory protection. Because the statute does not permit an evenhanded approach in which all individuals can claim disability discrimination, the courts have had to undermine the exclusive focus on people with disabilities by drastically limiting the scope of that class. Only a small subset of people with disabilities are eligible for the statute's antisubordination protection. One can therefore find a common anti-affirmative action thread running through both disability and race and sex antidiscrimination law in the United States, despite the differing statutory language.

## REASONABLE ACCOMMODATION CASE LAW

Title I of the ADA protects against employment discrimination of "qualified individuals with a disability." A "qualified individual with a disability" is a person with a disability who "with or without reasonable accommodation can perform the essential functions of the employment position such individual holds or desires." The term *reasonable accommodation* includes "reassignment to a vacant position." The controversy surrounding whether the ADA is an "affirmative action" statute has sometimes centered on that requirement. What priority, for example, might a person with a disability be entitled to over people seeking the same position? What obligation does an employer have to facilitate that reassignment? To the extent that the ADA is interpreted to require affirmative action such as priority consideration for a reassignment, it conflicts with hypercapitalism.

To understand the possible scope of the reassignment requirement, one first must understand it in the context of the ADA. The reasonable accommodation concept is part of the definition of a qualified individual with a disability. For example, if individual A has insulin-dependent diabetes, that individual usually is considered a person with a disability. If the person were seeking a job as a secretary, he or she might have to request periodic breaks during the day to take insulin injections. Those periodic breaks would be a "reasonable accommodation." Since the individual could perform the job with that reasonable accommodation, he or she becomes a qualified individual with a disability. Having met the criteria for a qualified individual with a disability, the person is also entitled to the statute's nondiscrimination protections. The employer could not, for example, fire all insulin-dependent diabetics (despite their ability to perform the job with a reasonable accommodation) and retain everyone else.

But now let us assume that the employer's needs change after the insulin-dependent diabetic is hired as a secretary. These changes mean that the diabetic will no longer be able to take the breaks that are essential to his or her safe functioning at the workplace. No reasonable accommodations at that particular worksite are possible to allow the person to be a qualified individual with a disability at his or her current job classification. According to Title I of the ADA, the employer nonetheless has an obligation to make the reasonable accommodation of "reassignment to a vacant position." This obligation is not defined as a nondiscrimination requirement but as a reasonable accommodation requirement.

The difference between a nondiscrimination requirement and a reasonable accommodation requirement is relevant to the concept of affirmative action. If the duty to reassign an employee to a vacant position were a *nondiscrimination* requirement, the employer could not discriminate against the secretary seeking to be reassigned after he or she becomes unqualified for his or her present position. The secretary would be given equal priority with other incumbent employees who sought reassignment. But if reassignment is a *reasonable accommodation*, then the employer's obligation is more than nondiscrimination; it must be an affirmative attempt to reassign the employee to a vacant position. The scope of that affirmative obligation, however, is not specified in the regulations or interpretive guidance, so it is unclear.

The cases construing the reassignment requirement have often restated the requirement as if it were a nondiscrimination rather than a reasonable accommodation requirement. For example, in *Daugherty v. City of El Paso*,[23] the Fifth Circuit found that the city's failure to reassign an insulin-dependent diabetic to another position on the city payroll did not violate its reasonable accommodation obligation under the ADA, "absent evidence that the city treated the employee differently from any other part-time employee whose job was eliminated." This holding, in fact, relied on a misstatement of the actual facts in *Daugherty*. Daugherty's job was not "eliminated"; rather, Daugherty was discharged from his job when his diabetes rendered him unqualified to comply with Department of Transportation rules for bus drivers. Because he had not been discharged for cause, he sought to take advantage of the reasonable accommodation/reassignment rule just described. The court described his situation as a job "elimination" in order to hide the disability aspects of his case.

In ruling against Daugherty on the reassignment issue, the court distinguished between nondiscrimination and affirmative action:

> Stated another way, we do not read the ADA as requiring affirmative action in favor of people with disabilities, in the sense of requiring that disabled persons be given priority in hiring or reassignment over those who are not disabled. It prohibits employment discrimination against qualified individuals with disabilities, no more and no less.

The court overlooked the fact that the reassignment/reasonable accommodation rule is a rule regarding priority consideration.

Similarly, in *Fussell v. Georgia Ports Authority*,[24] the district court concluded that the defendants did not violate the ADA when they failed to tell the plaintiff about an opening in another department, for which he may have been qualified, within ninety days of his disability-related discharge. The court granted the defendant's motion for summary judgment, concluding that no further factual inquiry was needed to assess liability, because it construed the reassignment/ reasonable accommodation rule to require no priority consideration.

In both cases, the courts glossed over the fact that the reassignment rule is contained in the reasonable accommodation section of the statute. The courts, however, did contend that it was the plaintiffs' lawyers, not the courts, who were misreading the ADA. As the *Fussell* court declared,

> [It is doubtful] whether Congress, in its wildest dreams or wildest nightmares, intended to turn every garden variety worker's compensation claim into a federal case. . . . [O]ne of the primary beneficiaries of [the ADA] will be trial lawyers who will ingeniously manipulate [the ADA's] ambiguities to consistently broaden its coverage so that federal courts may become mired in employment injury cases, becoming little more than glorified worker's compensation referees.[25]

But the *Fussell* court, like the *Daugherty* court, made misleading statements in order to arrive at its conclusion. The paragraph from its opinion just quoted was taken from another case, *Pedigo v. P.A.M. Transport, Inc.*,[26] and was taken completely out of context. In *Pedigo*, the plaintiff was a truck driver until he suffered a heart attack and underwent an angioplasty procedure. He was terminated while on medical leave. The jury found for the plaintiff because it concluded that the defendant had not sufficiently attempted to accommodate him by reassigning him to a vacant position. (Everyone agreed that he was no longer qualified to drive an over-the-road truck.) After the jury ruled in the plaintiff's favor, the defendant asked the court to overturn the verdict because the evidence was insufficient as a matter of law. As recited by the *Fussell* court, the district court in *Pedigo* did suggest that the ADA was not serving the public interest through its reassignment requirement. Nonetheless, after carefully examining the legislative history, the *Pedigo* court concluded that Congress did intend to require reassignment as a reasonable accommodation.

The *Fussell* court quoted *Pedigo* out of context to conclude that courts should narrowly construe the reassignment rule. The *Pedigo* court made this statement in the context of a reasonable accommodation/reassignment case in which it ruled in favor of the plaintiff. After examining the legislative history under the ADA, the *Pedigo* court ultimately decided: "[I]t appears that legislative history indicates that Congress intended to come down on the side of the administrative agencies which generally required the employer to consider reassignment, rather than on the side of the federal courts which had generally denied that the employer was obligated to do so."[27] The *Fussell* court relied on a deceptive citation to rule otherwise.

Many courts are therefore construing the ADA to erase the reassignment/reasonable accommodation rule. Rather than debate the proper scope of the reassignment requirement, they are pretending that the requirement does not exist at all. This is being done in the name of not making the ADA into an affirmative action statute. As we will see, Canada and Australia are more generous in interpreting this requirement in their statutes.

## SCOPE OF COVERAGE

*Introduction.* Because disability discrimination law explicitly requires reasonable accommodation, courts cannot dismantle its affirmative action elements entirely. But one technique that they can use to limit the scope of the disability discrimination law's affirmative action potential is to limit the scope of claimants permitted to bring suit. Thus, as we will see, the United States and Great Britain employ a much narrower understanding of who can bring suit for disability discrimination than do Canada and Australia. These differences are consistent with their differing versions of capitalism.

Two interpretations of the ADA have helped achieve a narrow understanding of who can bring a disability discrimination claim. First, some courts have used an exceedingly stringent test to determine whether a person has a substantial limitation in a major life activity. In particular, they have used a stringent test when the major life activity that is limited is the ability to work. Second, some courts have adopted a very restrictive test to determine whether the impairment is sufficiently substantial. They have evaluated the substantiality of the limitation after—rather than before—a person has used mitigating measures (for example, medication, eyeglasses, hearing aid, wheelchair). The first narrow interpretation is arguably supported by the regulatory language under the ADA, but the second interpretation flatly contradicts the regulations.

*Substantial Limitation in the Life Activity of Working.* The ADA typically provides coverage for a person who can demonstrate that he or she is substantially limited in a major life activity. Few would disagree that "working" is a major life activity, but the requirement of proof of a substantial limitation for this major life activity is more rigorous than for the other life activities specified in the regulations: "caring for oneself, performing manual tasks, walking, seeing, hearing, speaking, breathing,

[and] learning." The general regulation for substantial limitation is that the person is

> unable to perform a major life activity that the average person in the general population can perform; or significantly restricted as to the condition, manner or duration under which an individual can perform a particular major life activity as compared to the condition, manner, or duration under which the average person in the general population can perform that same major life activity.

With respect to the life activity of working, the regulations promulgated by the Equal Employment Opportunity Commission (EEOC) contain an additional requirement:

> The term substantially limits means significantly restricted in the ability to perform either a class of jobs or a broad range of jobs in various classes as compared to the average person having comparable training, skills and abilities. The inability to perform a single, particular job does not constitute a substantial limitation in the major life activity of working.

As an example of the application of this rule, the Interpretive Guidance explains that a professional baseball pitcher who has developed a bad elbow would be precluded from bringing a lawsuit under the ADA when he is no longer able to perform this highly specialized job. Common sense might suggest that when a person with extraordinary physical aptitude becomes disabled so that he can no longer perform at an extraordinarily high level of competence, he should be not be able to use the ADA to be characterized as "disabled." The EEOC therefore carved out this special rule with respect to the life activity of working to achieve this result, although the statute does not specify that "working" should be treated differently than other covered major life activities.

The EEOC, however, did not have to promulgate this special rule to reach that intended result. The ADA does not extend protection to all individuals with disabilities, only to *qualified* individuals with disabilities. If two people are applying for a job as a professional baseball pitcher and one person has an injured elbow that precludes him from pitching, the ADA would conclude that he was not a *qualified* individual with a disability (under the assumption that no reasonable accommodation would make him otherwise qualified). One would not even have to apply the major life activity of working rule to exclude him from statutory coverage. But if he were already working as a baseball pitcher when he injured his elbow, then it is true that the reassignment/reasonable accommodation rule would operate. Without the special major life activity rule, a baseball team might have to consider whether the pitcher could work at other positions or in the front office before discharging him from the organization. The major life activity rule, however, eliminates the need to apply the reassignment/reasonable accommodation rule, because the person is excluded from the definition of an individual with a disability.

Like the reassignment/reasonable accommodation rule, the major life activity of working rule is particularly detrimental to the job security of incumbent employees. The courts have also interpreted this requirement harshly to preclude many incumbent employees from obtaining the benefits of disability discrimination law. For example, in *Bolton v. Scrivner*,[28] the court awarded summary judgment to the defendants because the plaintiff failed to produce evidence that he could not perform a class of jobs. Bolton was not a baseball pitcher; he was an order selector in a grocery warehouse before he suffered a work-related injury to his feet. Although it is possible that a reasonable accommodation might have permitted Bolton to perform his job, the court of appeals ruled that the district court was correct in holding that "Bolton's inability to return to his particular job without some accommodation does not demonstrate a substantial limitation in the major life activity of working." He was excluded from the definition of an individual with a disability and therefore was not entitled to reasonable accommodation protection. Other persons who sought or held low-status jobs have been denied statutory coverage under such reasoning.[29] By relying on the special requirement for the major life activity of working, the courts have been able to avoid the more probing question of whether a reasonable accommodation might have permitted these people to maintain their jobs.

*Use of Mitigating Measures. Mitigating measures* are assistive devices (like a hearing aid, medication, wheelchair) that people use to lessen the effects of their disabilities on their daily functioning. An interpretive question under disability discrimination law is how one should determine whether an individual has a "substantial impairment of a major life activity," thereby meeting the definition of an individual with a disability before or after the use of mitigating measures. A broad definition of an individual with a disability would assess the degree of impairment *before* mitigating measures are used, whereas a narrow definition would assess the degree of impairment *after* mitigating measures are used.

Because the ADA is silent on this question, it has been resolved through EEOC regulations and judicial decisions. The EEOC has promulgated a broad rule: "The determination of whether an individual is substantially limited in a major life activity must be made on a case by case basis, without regard to mitigating measures such as medicines, or assistive or prosthetic devices." The EEOC offers no further guidance or examples regarding this rule. As we will see, some courts have rejected this broad rule.

Whether the substantiality of the limitation is determined before mitigating measures are used has important implications for the breadth of statutory coverage. Let us assume, for example, that a person works at a company that has a strict rule governing employee breaks. An employee has one fifteen-minute break in the morning, one half hour at lunchtime, and one fifteen-minute break in the afternoon. Let us further assume that an insulin-dependent diabetic employee cannot complete during these breaks all the monitoring and intake of food and insulin required for him or her to avoid diabetic symptoms. If we measured the substantiality of the impairment before the use of mitigating measures, this person would obviously be disabled. He or she would then be able to request a reasonable accommodation to facilitate the injection of insulin. But if we viewed the employee after the use of mitigating measures (although it is not even possible to use mitigating measures on that job), he or she might not have an opportunity to seek a modest reasonable accommodation.

The appropriateness of the EEOC's rule has repeatedly arisen in cases involving people with insulin-dependent diabetes.[30] In several recent cases, the courts have rejected the EEOC's mitigating measures rule and found that the plaintiffs had to place facts into evidence regarding the substantiality of their impairment after the use of mitigating measures.[31] In one of these cases, the court did not even permit the introduction of more evidence after the plaintiff relied on the EEOC guidelines for support that insulin-dependent diabetics are per se disabled because of their dependence on insulin in order to function. Rather, the court held that the plaintiff had not demonstrated that he was disabled.[32] In future cases, when plaintiffs are on notice that such evidence is necessary, the courts will have raised their litigation costs by making them put medical facts into evidence.

The rejection of the mitigating measures rule is just one more attempt to limit the category of people who can bring claims under the ADA. Rather than decide whether they genuinely have claims of discrimination—and many of them appeared to have very strong claims—the courts have closed the door of litigation in their face. No other country has adopted such a narrow mitigating measures rule.

*Other Narrowing Devices.* The ADA also narrows its statutory scope through more direct methods—by means of statutory exclusions. Title V of the ADA lists those conditions that are specifically excluded from coverage: homosexuality, bisexuality, transvestism, transsexualism, pedophilia, exhibitionism, voyeurism, gender identity disorders not resulting from physical impairments, other sexual behavior disorders, compulsive gambling, kleptomania, pyromania, psychoactive substance use disorders resulting from the current illegal use of drugs, and current illegal use of drugs. In addition, alcoholics can obtain only limited statutory coverage. Impairments are covered only if they are "substantial" and have a long-term effect on a person's life: "Advanced age, physical or personality characteristics, and environmental, cultural, and economic disadvantages are not impairments." Both Canada and Australia are much less restrictive in the list of disabilities covered by their statutes.

## Canada

### REASONABLE ACCOMMODATION CASE LAW

The Canadian constitution explicitly recognizes and protects affirmative action, and the Canadian Human Rights Act explicitly mentions that affirmative action is permitted:

> It is not a discriminatory practice for a person to adopt or carry out a special program, plan or arrangement designed to prevent disadvantages that are likely to be suffered by, or to eliminate or reduce advantages that are suffered by, any group of individuals when those disadvantages would be or are based on or related to the . . . disability of members of that group by improving opportunities respecting goods, services, facilities, accommodation or employment in relation to that group.[33]

Provincial legislation also contains similar protection. This language protects affirmative action programs from "reverse discrimination" challenges. Section 14(1) of the Ontario Human Rights Act, for example, provides that an equality right is "not infringed by the implementation of a special program designed to relieve hardship or economic disadvantage or assist disadvantaged persons or groups to achieve or attempt to achieve equal opportunity or that is likely to contribute to the elimination of the infringement of rights under Part I." The Ontario Court of Appeal interpreted these provisions to mean that a "reverse discrimination" claim cannot be made under Canadian law, although one could challenge a disability affirmative action program for discriminating against another disadvantaged group.[34]

Ironically, however, the Canadian disability discrimination statute (which is part of its general human rights statute) does not explicitly require reasonable accommodation. That duty was impliedly found to exist in the 1980s in cases involving religious, age, and pregnancy discrimination.[35] Despite the absence of an explicit statutory requirement to reasonably accommodate, Canadian courts have been more generous than U.S. courts in interpreting the reasonable accommodation/reassignment rule in cases involving disability discrimination.

Reflecting on the federal disability discrimination legislation in Canada, Brian Doyle described the scope of reasonable accommodation more narrowly than I did: "Although employers are permitted to take special action to prevent, eliminate or reduce disadvantage faced by disabled individuals in employment opportunities, this provides blessing only to voluntarily conceded reasonable accommodation."[36] Relying on religious discrimination case law involving the duty of reasonable accommodation from the United States, Doyle speculated that the Canadian courts will interpret the reasonable accommodation requirement narrowly in the disability context. The religious cases from the United States, however, offer the courts very different problems because of their special constitutional status. In the United States, the courts have resisted importing the religious reasonable accommodation rulings into disability discrimination law.

An illuminating example of the liberal Canadian approach to reasonable accommodation is *Re Province of Manitoba and Manitoba Government Employees' Union*.[37] A union filed a grievance regarding an employee's right to be reassigned after he was no longer able to perform the duties of his position. (The applicable Human Rights Code states that discrimination means the "failure to make reasonable accommodation for the special needs of any individual or group, if those special needs are based upon any [disability] characteristic.")[38] The grievant, Mr. Ulasy, became disabled and was informed that he would be given priority consideration for other vacant positions in the civil service. Both the plaintiff and the defendant agreed that reassignment as a form of affirmative action was appropriate, so the dispute centered on the scope of that preferential treatment. Although the defendant government had interviewed the grievant for several positions, the arbitrator concluded that further steps to accommodate him were required. The arbitrator required the defendants to conduct a more up-to-date medical assessment of the plaintiff's abilities to perform job-related tasks, with consideration given to medical rehabilitation or retraining; to look at necessary modifications of job positions before the plaintiff's interview for a particular position; and to consider a trial period for a new position to assess whether the plaintiff was qualified to perform it. The arbitrator concluded that such proposals might allow the plaintiff to compete on a more "level playing field." In other words, affirmative action would create equal opportunity. This case is reflective of Canada's liberal approach to the reassignment rule.[39] Although reassignment is not listed in the Canadian statute as an example of reasonable accommodation, arbitrators have gone quite far in dictating of what the duty consists, as long as it is not an undue hardship. Although required by statute to consider reassignment as a reasonable accommodation, the American courts have offered a much narrower interpretation of that rule.

## SCOPE OF STATUTORY COVERAGE

The coverage of people with disabilities is much broader in Canada than in the United States. For example, the Ontario

Human Rights Code, which includes protection against handicap discrimination, does not contain the "substantial impairment" language found in American law. The Canadian statute defines "because of handicap" to include a person who has, has had, or is believed to have had

> any degree of physical disability, infirmity, malformation or disfigurement that is caused by bodily injury, birth defect or illness—a condition of mental retardation or impairment, a learning disability or a dysfunction in one or more of the processes involving in understanding or using symbols or spoken language, a mental disorder, or an injury or disability for which benefits were claimed or received under the Workers' Compensation Act.[40]

(This language is in direct contrast to the American courts that have resisted making the ADA into an expanded worker's compensation statute.) The "any degree" language is much broader than the "substantial impairment of a major life activity" language found in American law. Similarly, the Canadian Human Rights Act quite broadly defines people with a disability and specifically lists "previous or existing dependence on alcohol or a drug."[41]

In addition, the Ontario code specifically lists disabilities included under that definition: "diabetes mellitus, epilepsy, any degree of paralysis, amputation, lack of physical coordination, blindness or visual impairment, deafness or hearing impediment, muteness or speech impediment, or physical reliance on a guide dog or on a wheelchair or other remedial appliance or device." Obviously, insulin-dependent diabetics can obtain coverage under the Ontario statute. There is also little question that the issue of whether one is handicapped is measured *before* the use of mitigating measures because a dependence on mitigating measures makes one disabled.

Not surprisingly, the case law in Ontario reflects this broad definition. One arbitrator presumed that a person who suffers from kleptomania would be covered by the law,[42] whereas another arbitrator concluded that an alcoholic was covered by the Ontario statute by referring to the more specific language from the Canadian Human Rights Act concerning the coverage of alcoholics.[43]

### Great Britain

#### REASONABLE ACCOMMODATION CASE LAW

In Great Britain, affirmative action (or what is usually called *positive action*) is not currently a well-favored principle in the area of race or gender discrimination. Thus, the concept of reasonable accommodation is narrowly defined under Great Britain's new disability discrimination legislation. Great Britain's fifty-year statutory quota system, in which employers were obliged by law to maintain a 3 percent quota of people with disabilities in their workforces, was repealed when the antidiscrimination provisions of Part 2 of the new disability discrimination statutes took effect in 1996.[44]

It is too early to know how the courts will interpret the recently enacted disability rules in Great Britain, but it does appear that the statute presumes a narrow interpretation of reasonable accommodation. The British statute calls a reasonable accommodation an "adjustment" and states that when arrangements or physical feature place the disabled person at a *substantial* disadvantage in comparison with persons who are not disabled, it is the duty of the employer to take such steps as it is reasonable, in all the circumstances of the case, for him to take in order to prevent the arrangements or feature having that effect.

The statute offers the following examples of such "arrangements" that relate to reassignment: "transferring him to fill an existing vacancy" and "assigning him to a different place of work." By limiting the transfer to an existing vacancy, the British model certainly seems less generous than the Canadian model, which seems to entail extensive consideration for reassignment over a lengthy time period. The British model is also more attentive to cost considerations, although the details of the regulations have yet to be worked out. By being attentive to costs and offering a narrow scope of reasonable accommodation, the British model appears to be deferential to the needs of employers in a capitalistic society, reflecting the conservative political regime that enacted the legislation. In addition, the British statute explicitly states that it is not intended to require preferential or favorable treatment for a person with a disability.

Nonetheless, people with disabilities might be reassigned in Great Britain under the general principles of employment law. Under British common law the employment-at-will principle has eroded, so that most employees with at least two years of work experience are protected against being laid off if they become disabled once on the job. There is therefore a seeming conflict between Great Britain's recent enactment of disability discrimination protection and its preexisting common law protection for all workers. The current disability law mirrors the conservative economic influences in Great Britain, and the common law reflects earlier support for the labor movement.

## SCOPE OF STATUTORY COVERAGE

The recently enacted British statute is even narrower than the U.S. statute in providing coverage to people with disabilities. The effect of a disability must be both "substantial" and "long term" and must affect "normal day-to-day activities." There is no "record of" or "regarded as" expansion of this definition, as there is in the United States. In addition, Schedule 1 of the act provides for further limitation of impairments that may qualify as disabilities. The British Disability Discrimination Act of 1995 defines a disability as "a physical or mental impairment which has a substantial and long-term adverse effect on his ability to carry out normal day-to-day activities." For example, a mental impairment "includes an impairment resulting from or consisting of a mental illness only if the illness is a clinically well-recognized illness." Nonetheless, the British statute clearly states that a court should consider whether one is disabled *before* the effect of mitigating measures is taken into consideration, unless the corrective measures are spectacles or contact lenses. "An impairment which would be likely to have a substantial adverse effect on the ability of the person concerned to carry out normal day-to-day activities, but for the fact that measures are being taken to treat or correct it, is to be treated as having that effect." Thus, even the conservative British Parliament rejected the mitigating measures rule adopted by some courts in the United States.

## **Australia**

### REASONABLE ACCOMMODATION

The case law from Australia with respect to reasonable accommodation is still at an early stage and so is somewhat hard to evaluate. In an early case interpreting the disability discrimination law of New South Wales, the supreme court was very deferential to an employer's assertion as to what constitutes a "reasonable" accommodation in an employment application case.[45] Nonetheless, more recent decisions appear to be deferring much less to employer's assertions concerning the economics of its workforce.[46]

### SCOPE OF STATUTORY COVERAGE

The Australian Disability Discrimination Act of 1992 defines disability broadly:

> (a) total or partial loss of the person's bodily or mental functions; or (b) total or partial loss of a part of the body; or (c) the presence in the body of organisms causing disease or illness; or (d) the presence in the body or organisms capable of causing disease or illness; or (e) the malfunction, malformation or disfigurement of a part of the person's body; or (f) a disorder or malfunction that results in the person learning differently from a person without the disorder or malfunction; or (g) a disorder, illness or disease that affects a person's thought processes, perception of reality, emotions or judgment or that results in disturbed behavior; and includes a disability that; (h) presently exists; or (i) previously existed but no longer exists; or (j) may exist in the future; or (k) is imputed to a person.[47]

Unlike the ADA's requirement, the disability need not substantially limit a major life activity. Proving the existence of an impairment that fits into one of seven categories is sufficient for coverage. In addition, protection exists for people for whom the disability currently exists, previously existed but no longer exists, may exist in the future, or is imputed. Australian courts appear to be applying these definitions broadly.[48]

The breadth of statutory coverage in these four countries therefore corresponds to the strength of their reasonable accommodation protection. Great Britain has the narrowest definition of disability and the most limited reasonable accommodation protection. Canada and Australia offer broad reasonable accommodation protection and, accordingly, offer a broad definition of disability. The United States offers a broader definition than does Great Britain, as well as broader reasonable accommodation protection, but is narrower on both grounds than is Canada or Australia.

One might say that it is ironic that countries with broad definitions of disability offer broad reasonable accommodation protection because this combination could be quite expensive for employers. This trend, however, does fit my thesis with regard to a willingness to apply principles that are somewhat inconsistent with hypercapitalism. Countries that are willing to act inconsistently with extreme laissez-faire economics offer broad protection at every turn; they do not seek to accommodate the employer's cost considerations.

One might argue that the American courts are correct to offer such a narrow definition of a person with a disability because such a narrow definition is consistent with American law and economics. But the fact that even Great Britain offers a considerably broader definition of a person with a disability should make a conservative jurist pause for further reflection. Through the adoption of the ADA, even the Republican-dominated Congress probably intended to provide meaningful protection to people with a disability. But, for example, excluding insulin-dependent diabetics from statutory coverage is not consistent with such intentions.

Remarkably, the ADA was passed by a bipartisan Congress. Even more remarkably, it is framed on an antisubordination approach that grants rights only to people with disabilities. Despite the hostility of many employers to affirmative action, it goes much further than Title VII in ordering employers to make reasonable accommodations for people with disabilities.

The backlash has been quick and decisive. The scope of the reasonable accommodation obligation has been narrowed far beyond the statutory language, and the categories of people who can bring claims under the statute has been confined beyond the intentions of Congress or the EEOC. Moreover, conservative newspapers have fueled this backlash by exaggerating the scope of success for claimants under the ADA.

Why has there been this quick backlash to a congressional bipartisan effort? Capitalism cannot accommodate affirmative action even when race and gender issues are not at stake. In Canada, most disability cases are decided as arbitrator decisions involving union grievances on behalf of disabled employees. The labor contracts typically contain their own protection for workers who become disabled and thereby serve to strengthen the applicable disability statute. Since a strong labor movement is indicative of a more socialist economy, it is consistent with my thesis that these arbitration decisions protect people with disabilities, often providing them with what I have termed affirmative action protection.

What type of state intervention best serves the interests of people with disabilities? To begin to answer that question, we must recognize that many different forms of state intervention existing in this area of the law deserve close examination. America's parochial lens often prevents such a wide-ranging analysis.

# 4

## FAMILY AND MEDICAL LEAVE

Kimberly Hern Troupe was employed as a saleswoman in the women's accessories department at Lord & Taylor.[1] She experienced extreme nausea while pregnant and frequently reported to work late or had to leave early. Although her employment record had been perfect before she became pregnant, she was fired the day before her maternity leave was to commence. Troupe brought suit alleging that her employer fired her because of her pregnancy and would have tolerated a similar illness if experienced by a male employee. Her lawsuit was unsuccessful, with the court blaming Troupe for her nausea, seemingly buying the stereotype that nausea occurs during pregnancy only in the morning. Thus, the court of appeals—in a decision written by Judge Richard Posner—blames her for the "morning sickness" by suggesting that she caused it to last until noon "because she slept later under the new schedule, so that noon was 'morning' for her."

The *Troupe* decision is typical of the hostility that U.S. courts have shown to suits brought by pregnant women. Rejecting the notion that pregnancy-based discrimination is based on sex, U.S. courts have refused to consider such discrimination as part of the constitutional law of sex discrimination.[2] Other countries, such as Canada, have, however, incorporated pregnancy discrimination cases into the law of sex discrimination.[3] And when the Pregnancy Discrimination Act (PDA)[4] was passed to specify that pregnancy-based discrimination in employment should be considered sex-based discrimination, some U.S. courts imposed impossible burdens of proof on female plaintiffs.[5] Other courts have used the PDA as an opportunity to rule for male plaintiffs, overturning "special treatment" rules for pregnant women.[6] U.S. antidiscrimination law has not given pregnant women much substantive protection, regardless of the content of such laws, especially when the cases have been decided by judges who are sympathetic to extreme laissez-faire arguments.

U.S. law also does little to protect fetuses from hazards at the workplace while women are pregnant. Federal antidiscrimination law requires no accommodations for pregnant women. Interpretations of the PDA combined with interpretations of the Occupational Safety and Health Act[7] (OSHA) have resulted in no meaningful federal guidelines to make the workplace safe for fetuses. Instead, the private marketplace sets standards in this area in the name of laissez-faire economics. Canada and western Europe, by contrast, have found ways to accommodate both the health of the fetus and the rights of the pregnant worker.

Finally, the United States stands alone in the Western world in failing to require employers to provide paid maternity leave following the birth of a child. Until 1993, South Africa and the United States were the only industrialized nations that did not have a federal maternity or parental leave policy.[8] Until quite recently, women who took unpaid medical leave following the birth of a child could be fired. After nearly a decade of political struggle, women who work for large employers are now entitled to twelve weeks of unpaid leave following the birth or adoption of a child,[9] which provides few genuine options for the over-whelming number of poor or even middle-class women who cannot afford to take unpaid leave and still pay the bills. Their only solace is that *if they work for a large employer*, they at least will have a job to which they can return after taking the most minimal possible medical leave.

The limited protections for pregnant women in the United States have received strong criticism from the leaders of laissez-faire economics. On the issue of legally imposed "special treatment" for pregnant women under antidiscrimination law, Professor Richard Epstein commented,

> Because pregnancy is desired, and because women largely control whether and when to become pregnant, the evident moral hazard makes pregnancy a poor candidate for any form of insurance. . . . The legislative and judicial insistence on their [pregnancy's] special status, however, cannot obscure the social losses incurred by their implementation, with pregnancy as elsewhere.[10]

He further criticizes the Pregnancy Discrimination Act as using "the antidiscrimination norm as a tool for redistributive ends." Epstein wrote those words in response to the use of antidiscrimination law for the benefit of pregnant women; one can only imagine what he might say about a blatantly preferential treatment policy like the Family Medical and Leave Act (FMLA).

Economic discourse has dominated the discussion of the treatment of pregnant women in the United States. Will social welfare programs cause poor women to bear more children? (While the United States seeks to limit the amount of financial support to poor women with children, many European countries continue their subsidization program for all families with children. For example, Germany provides monthly benefits of approximately $395 per month to the family until the child reaches six months and then offers a somewhat reduced benefit until the child reaches twenty-four months. Another program then provides a subsidy until a child reaches the age of twenty-seven months.)[11] Would mandated insurance coverage, paid leave, or accommodations for pregnancy bankrupt businesses? Based on few empirical data but much speculation by law and economics scholars, the free-market proponents have largely won the debate in the United States. Any scheme of pregnancy-related benefits or accommodations is largely a matter of bargaining between employees and employers, because the government has imposed few standards in this area.

This discussion is uniquely American for two reasons. First, it is dominated by the discourse of laissez-faire economics. Second, it virtually ignores the needs and interests of young children. (Even when authors argue that men should have more access to parental leave, they speak from the perspective of how such leave benefits the parents—that is, it gives men an opportunity to develop parenting skills and alleviates women's disproportionate child care burden—rather than from the perspective of how such leave benefits the children.)[12] Health insurance for pregnant women results in increased access to prenatal care which in turn reduces the incidence of low-birth-weight babies. Paid leave for parents also facilitates breast-feeding and parental care for the first year of a child's life.

There is ample evidence that nearly all forms of nonparental care in the first year of life are inferior to the care offered by good parents.[13] Yet the United States has taken no steps to improve the quality of nonparental care offered to infants or to help parents provide that care themselves. This second problem can also be attributed to the negative effects of capitalism on American life. The free-market, autonomy principles underlying American capitalism prevent us from being "other directed" in our consideration of social problems. It is as if we have forgotten that pregnant women usually give birth at the end of their pregnancies. The short period of medical leave that they might receive after the birth of a child does not even begin to address the needs of the infant who has just been born and is in his or her most dependent, and possibly most important, stage of development.

The discourse in other countries, even other capitalist countries, has been vastly different. The needs of pregnant women are built around the understanding that a child will soon be born who needs special assistance. When a society offers assistance to parents in the form of paid leave, insurance, or accommodations away from workplace hazards, the real beneficiaries of that assistance should be considered the child, not the pregnant woman. The whole "special treatment" debate in the United States has been warped by a misunderstanding of who receives and needs that special treatment.

Throughout U.S. history, we have always lumped together "women and children" in our discourse as if they were a unitary entity and as if the woman herself needed paternalistic protection. This tradition continues in our modern discourse about pregnancy discrimination and pregnancy leave. In this chapter, I try to separate the needs of pregnant women and children to argue that special treatment is and should be offered to the newly born child (or the fetus *in utero*). It is conceptually wrong to view that treatment as having been extended to the pregnant woman.

## The Economic Debate

Economic discourse has dominated the arguments both for and against paid parenting leave and health insurance coverage for pregnant women. Richard Epstein's discussion of mandated insurance coverage for pregnant women rests entirely on economic arguments concerning the stability of voluntary insurance systems. He contends that disability insurance systems will inevitably "disintegrate" if coverage for pregnancy is required; therefore, it is in everyone's interest to exclude pregnancy in order to maintain the viability of the insurance disability market.[14] According to his economic analysis, any insurance system that covers pregnancy should falter because women would then choose to become pregnant and so take advantage of these programs, thereby creating a substantial increased cost that would undermine the system's economic viability. Epstein's arguments are entirely theoretical—he offers no empirical support connecting the availability of any of these benefits and women's behavior. His theoretical arguments are based on his initial assumption that "pregnancy is desired, and . . . women largely control whether and when to become pregnant."[15] Similarly, The *Wall Street Journal* regularly publishes editorials ridiculing the FMLA, with headlines such as "Family-Leave Law Can Be

Excuse for a Day Off."[16] These articles complain that the $674 million price tag for the statute, as predicted by the General Accounting Office, will be much higher in practice.

Judge Richard Posner has made no secret of his hostility to the PDA and mandated maternity leave in his academic writings, arguing that the PDA may not even benefit most women.[17] Nonetheless, Posner is forced to acknowledge that the cost of laws such as the PDA may be offset "by gains not measured in an economic analysis—gains in self-esteem." Never does he consider, however, whether the benefits of such laws might be measured in the well-being of our next generation. His failure to consider this argument is somewhat surprising because he does seem fascinated with romantic notions of women's maternal role. For example, he states earlier in the article:

> It is possible that the greater propensity of women than men to take time out of the labor force is itself a product of sex discrimination, but I am skeptical of that proposition—I think child-rearing is an area where nature dominates culture—and I do not accept it for purposes of my analysis.[18]

Not surprisingly, Posner's hostility to the PDA is reflected in his decisions as a jurist, although some economists have misunderstood Posner's position on the PDA. For example, Irving Michelman, a former corporate executive and adviser to the Federal Reserve Board and the U.S. Department of Commerce, cites Posner's dissent in *International Union v. Johnson Controls*[19] as reflecting a "morally-based, efficiency alternative" which would "find a way to interpret anti-discrimination laws . . . to include fetal protection."[20] Michelman suggests that Posner's analysis reflects his sensitivity to the business community as well as to fetal safety and women's welfare. How he reaches that conclusion from Posner's analysis, however, is hard to fathom.

The issue in the case was whether an employer could prevent all fertile women from working in its battery-manufacturing plant in a position with a high exposure to lead. Completely ignoring the Pregnancy Discrimination Act (PDA), the majority concluded that such a policy was lawful. The U.S. Supreme Court ultimately reversed the district court and court of appeals, concluding that the policy was a pregnancy-based distinction that expressly violated the PDA.

Although Judge Posner dissented from the opinion of the court of appeals, his opinion hardly reflects much concern for the position of women at the workplace. He prefaces his analysis with the assumption taken from Gary Becker's 1971 book, *The Economics of Discrimination*, that "few private employers discriminate without having some reason for doing so; competition tends to drive from the market firms that behave irrationally."[21] But Becker's assessment depends on a full-employment economy and certainly does not apply to low-level jobs at a battery plant where the pool of workers is enormous. (The presumably rational employer in this case assumed that any woman under the age of seventy is fertile!) Unlike the majority opinion, Posner does actually acknowledge that Title VII was amended in 1982 to include the Pregnancy Discrimination Amendment, which defined sex discrimination to include discrimination on the basis of pregnancy. Nonetheless, he refuses to interpret this amendment liberally (consistent, as we will see, with all his interpretations of the PDA) to forbid an employer to deal with the problem of safety at the workplace by refusing to hire fertile women. Instead, he says that an employer should be able to show evidence of the potential cost of tort liability, moral qualms about endangering the child, or the effect on public relations of revealing the safety hazards at its workplace. Thus, Posner suggests that the court should remand the case back to the district court "to enable the compilation of an adequate evidentiary record."

Even though Posner indicates that this defense is a narrow one, one would expect the district court judge in this case to rule once again for the defendant employer. After all, the district court, with sparse evidence on a summary judgment motion, had already ruled once for the employer, so with additional evidence, one would expect the district court to rule once more for the defendant. (The Supreme Court sidestepped this possibility by ruling authoritatively for the plaintiffs, without leaving open the possibility of a victory for the defendant employer on remand.) Nonetheless, Posner is praised by an economist who does not seem to appreciate that Posner virtually never reaches legal decisions that protect the employment interests of pregnant women. As we will see when we examine the policies of other countries, there are far better solutions to this problem than Posner's, based not on the presumed economic rationality of employers but on the importance of safeguarding both women's economic security and the health of the fetus.

Arguments supporting increased benefits for pregnant women also often speak in purely economic terms. For example, Samuel Issacharoff and Elyse Rosenblum cite President Clinton's "nannygate" episode in trying to find a qualified (female) attorney general as exemplifying the need for a national maternity policy that can accommodate the needs of working women.[22] "[W]ithout accommodation for pregnancy, women experience an elevated level of early departure from the work force and an associated failure to develop what economists term job specific capital—that is, the enhanced skills and productivity that come from experience on the job." Exploring the relationship between wages and continuous workplace participation, they insist that the United States needs a model similar to the one used in Canada so that women would receive unemployment insurance for twelve weeks postpartum so long as they had worked for their employer for at least ten weeks before becoming pregnant. Unlike Epstein, they base their proposal on empirical evidence connecting women's childbearing decisions and the availability of insurance systems. But unlike Epstein, they do not presume that women have children in order to collect pregnancy leave benefits. Having begun with a different premise, they arrive at a different economic solution. (My survey of the existing statistics on birthrates, pregnancy leave policies, and women's participation in the workforce suggests no connection among these factors. German and Italy, for example, which have generous pregnancy-based policies also have the lowest birthrates in Europe—ten per one thousand population—compared with the United States' relatively high birthrate—sixteen per one thousand population.)[23]

Issacharoff and Rosenblum's program would certainly improve women's economic situation following the birth of a child but is unlikely to have any appreciable impact on the "nannygate" problem that introduces their article. The women with "nanny" problems were not impeded in their careers by a lack of compensation for twelve weeks of pregnancy leave. In March 1986, Kimba Wood hired an illegal alien from Trinidad to care for her infant son. The employment was actually lawful because at that time, federal law permitted illegal aliens to be hired in such positions. Furthermore, the nanny became a legal resident in 1987, thus allowing Wood to continue to employ her legally. Wood also paid all required Social Security taxes on the nanny's wages. She worked for the family for many years, permitting both Wood and her husband to continue working in time-consuming and highly paid positions.[24] The political reaction against Wood can most likely be explained by the fact that she hired a non-American, not that she acted in an unlawful manner. Wood's career, however, was certainly not impeded, as Issacharoff and Rosenblum suggest, because she could not take sufficient medical leave following the birth of her son. Similarly, Zoe Baird and her husband hired a foreign couple as a babysitter and driver for a lengthy period of time. The couple were obviously alleviating the burdens of combining paid employment and child care, but their presence was not for the purpose of alleviating a short-term need for medical leave following the birth of a child.

Understanding the importance of continuous workplace participation to success in high-powered careers, these women took a minimal break from the workplace following the birth of their children. Their "nanny" problems were caused by their limited options for high-quality care for their children after they returned to paid employment. Like many parents, they concluded that a group child care situation was not optimal in the first year of so of their child's life. That left them with two choices: the parents could work out a schedule that permitted them to stay home with the child, or they could hire someone else to come into their home to take care of the child. Even though either option is much more expensive for most parents than group day care, many parents make the (uneconomical) decision to use one of these arrangements. Why?

Laissez-faire economics cannot provide an answer here. Parents, who supposedly decide to have children depending on the disability insurance scheme available for the six weeks following the birth of their child, are also making blatantly uneconomical decisions—they are paying more than $1,000 per month to someone else to take care of their child or forgoing at least that much money in income by taking care of the child themselves rather than paying about $500 per month for group care for their child. The answer is that parents do not make child care (or pregnancy) decisions on a purely economic basis. If they did consider economics seriously, most adults, of course, would forgo parenting altogether. But even after deciding to partake of the psychic and emotional rewards of parenting, they do not always seek to minimize the costs of parenting. That is, they sometimes choose highly uneconomical options in the early years of a child's life out of their concern for the child's well-being. This enduring fact will survive any tinkering with the paid leave policy in the United States. It will endure because even in this highly capitalistic society, parents are and will be motivated by forces other than economics.

Poor women's decisions can also be understood as reflecting decisions about child care rather than about economics. Some working-class women who earn the minimum wage find that it makes more sense to quit their jobs and go on welfare after the birth of a child than to stay at paid work. With the inadequate system of child care and health insurance that is available to poor women, staying at home to raise their child is the only way to safeguard their child's well-being. Their decisions parallel the decisions sometimes made by upper-class women—that is, they choose an uneconomical option in order to safeguard the well-being of their children. The language of the welfare debate, however, condemns them as bad mothers without understanding the rationality of their decisions from the perspective of the child's well-being.

The proposal offered by Issacharoff and Rosenblum has, in fact, few similarities to the actual scope of leave benefits available in Canada. In 1990, Bill C-21 became federal law in Canada, thereby creating fifteen weeks of maternity benefits for the biological mother and a ten-week parenting benefit that could be taken by either parent.[25] (The provinces have their own parallel statutes governing some employment not covered by the federal statute. In Ontario, for example, the Employment Standards Act entitles a woman to take seventeen weeks of pregnancy leave and either parent to take eighteen weeks of parental leave.)[26] Canadian parents receive compensation for nearly six months of leave following the birth of a child, not the twelve weeks proposed by Issacharoff and Rosenblum. Parents can also take their benefits on a part-time basis, spreading them out over fifty-two weeks. Finally, a portion of this leave is available to either parent; the justification is not simply the biological needs of the pregnant woman. The effect of the Canadian legislation is to help enable parents to care for their children themselves for the first six months and possibly first year of life. It is the interests of the young child, not the pregnant woman, that justify such a lengthy leave period for either parent.

European law is often comparable to the law of Canada in helping parents take paid leave for much of the child's first year of life. For example, Italy passed its Equal Treatment Act (ETA) in 1977, which built on the preexisting 1971 maternity law and provided the following benefits to new parents: a three-month leave for the mother at 80 percent pay after the birth or adoption of a child and an optional six-month additional leave that can be taken by either parent at 30 percent pay.[27] Working mothers were also guaranteed rest periods during the first year of a child's life.

Owing to legal action in 1987, Italian law was soon equalized to provide more comparable benefits for male and female parents. The plaintiffs were fathers of newborn children whose mothers had died in childbirth or were infirm and immobilized. These men successfully argued that they, too, should be entitled to the three-month postpartum leave and rest periods in accordance with the law of equal treatment. In ruling for the male plaintiffs, the Constitutional Court noted that the rationale of the maternity law reflected a growing public concern "for the child's affective and psychological well-being as well as its biological needs." Although the maternity law may have been initially passed in 1950 out of a concern for the frailty of pregnant women and a desire to make breast-feeding easier, its current structure reflects an increasing concern for the welfare of the young child. As a result of another legal challenge in 1991, by a father whose wife was healthy but did not want to take the three-month leave to care for the child, the Constitutional Court again ruled that the statute's protections must be extended to fathers. The court recognized that the purpose of the legislation was to address the "relational and affective needs that are connected to the development of the personality of the child."[28] The purely biological justifications for the legislation were outmoded.

Nearly every European country provides women with at least eight weeks of paid leave following the birth of a child, which is then followed by a period of paid parental leave.[29] It is clear from the language of these statutes that even the maternity leave is justified in part by the needs of the child. For example, in Germany, Norway, Poland, and Luxembourg, maternity leave is lengthened if the baby is born prematurely or the woman has a multiple birth. Some countries, like Poland, also lengthen the maternity leave if there is already another child in the household. And unlike the United States, none of the European countries exempts small businesses from statutory coverage.

Suggestions that the United States move toward a paid system of leave following the birth of a child produces the following kind of reaction from economic conservatives:

> What we need is another welfare scheme, this one for job holders. What a concept. Now, push the baby carriage down to the FMLA office and pick up your "wage replacement" check once a week for the next three months. Maybe they'll electronically mail it to your banking account. Is this country great, or what? Insane, comes to mind.[30]

By contrast, Professor Edward Zigler, who lobbied in favor of a bill that would have required a six-month paid leave for new parents describes the FMLA act as "awful." "It's especially awful when you stop to consider that Ghana has a paid leave; Haiti has a paid leave, for God's sake. When are we going to join the rest of the world?"[31] One's version of what's "insane" seems to depend on one's view of economics and consideration of the well-being of children. Only in the United States is the requirement that employers offer paid leave to parents following the birth or adoption of a child considered to be insane.

### Special Treatment/Equal Treatment Discourse

A second key aspect of the pregnancy debate in the United States is its focus on the special treatment/equal treatment issue. The question that has been posed for nearly a century is whether mandated leave legislation following the birth of a child will help or hinder women's position in society. This argument, like the economic one just discussed, has largely ignored the needs and interests of the young child. Instead, it presumes that the woman rather than the fetus or young child is receiving the special treatment.

### PROTECTING THE CHILD AFTER BIRTH

*Equal Treatment Cases.* The Pregnancy Discrimination Act has generally been interpreted to incorporate an equal treatment rather than a special treatment model. In doing so, the act sometimes helps prevent overt discrimination against pregnant women but never helps accommodate the needs of the child following birth. A case that reflects this pattern is *Maganuco v. Leyden Community High School District 212*.[32] Plaintiff Maganuco was a pregnant schoolteacher who wanted to use her accumulated paid sick leave before taking an unpaid maternity leave. But school policy forbid someone who took maternity leave to combine it with paid sick leave. Maganuco argued that this rule violated the PDA by creating a disparate impact against women in the workplace. Drawing a distinction between the plaintiff's medical needs and her child care needs, the court ruled against the plaintiff:

> Teachers who choose not to take maternity leave, and decide instead to return to teaching as soon as their period of pregnancy-related disability ends, are unaffected by the policy that Maganuco challenges. The impact of the leave policy that Maganuco contests, then, is dependent not on the biological fact that pregnancy and childbirth cause some period of disability, but on a Leyden schoolteacher's choice to forego

returning to work in favor of spending time at home with her newborn child. However, this choice is not the inevitable consequence of a medical condition related to pregnancy, and leave policies that may influence the decision to remain at home after the period of pregnancy-related disability has ended fall outside the scope of the PDA.[33]

The Seventh Circuit's description of Maganuco's "choice" to stay home with her newborn baby makes it sound like she is staying home to play games. (Maybe the court should also have mentioned her "choice" in not relinquishing the child for adoption so that she would not have any child care needs at all.) Earlier in its opinion, the court described Maganuco as needing only "10 days of post-delivery recuperation" to recover from her pregnancy. Presumably, she should then have returned to work full time, although no day care center will even consider taking a child until he or she is at least six weeks old. Once ten days have passed and her medical needs have supposedly ended, the PDA's concern for the new mother's treatment at the workplace expires. This uncaring and callous consideration of the needs of the newborn and the new mother is entirely possible in the equal treatment regime of the United States, in which we can overlook the fact that most pregnant women give birth to a child who will have significant child care needs.

Canadian courts have reached the opposite conclusion based on similar facts. Canadian plaintiff Carlinda D'Alimonte also was a pregnant schoolteacher who wanted to combine sick leave and maternity leave following the birth of her child, in violation of her company's personnel policies.[34] A board of arbitration upheld the employer's position. But on appeal, the Ontario Divisional Court concluded that such a coerced choice violated the law against sex discrimination. Citing an earlier decision by the Canadian Supreme Court, the Ontario court emphasized that a finding of discrimination was necessary in order to redress a basic disadvantage that women face at the workplace and in society at large. "It [the rule] would sanction imposing a disproportionate amount of the costs of pregnancy upon women. Removal of such unfair impositions upon women and other groups in society is a key purpose of anti-discrimination legislation." The Ontario court viewed pregnancy as benefiting society as a whole and so expected employers and society as a whole to bear some of those costs. Rather than viewing the plaintiff's pregnancy as a private choice, the court viewed it in the context of mutual social responsibility.

Until the passage of the Family and Medical Leave Act, federal law in the United States provided no protection for workers who needed to miss work because of illness or because of family responsibilities such as child care. Canadian law, by contrast, offers protection to workers under both its antidiscrimination law (both disability and sex-based law) and its generous parenting leave law. Furthermore, workers are often protected under collective-bargaining agreements that do not permit them to be discharged for illness-related leave unless the employer can demonstrate that the employee is incapable of regular attendance in the future.[35]

Canada and the United States operate under different premises regarding the role of the state in workers' lives. Canada is accustomed to intervening, under its version of capitalism, to provide minimum levels of protections for workers, whereas the United States does so quite begrudgingly. For example, in a typical Canadian case involving a union grievance, the arbitrator deferred to the judgment of the employee's physician while recognizing that the "evidence places the grievor on the borderline and it may turn out to have been too optimistic."[36] A U.S. court is unlikely to interpret a close case in favor of the employee.

The only federal statute that applies a "special accommodation" principle—the Americans with Disabilities Act—does not cover such requests by pregnant women because pregnancy is a "normal" rather than "disabling" condition.[37] Federal law thereby imposes no standards on the workplace to enable women to give birth to healthy newborns who will then, in turn, have an opportunity to obtain good care in the first year of life. Because there are no nonpregnant employees with comparable responsibilities for another's life, employers are permitted to ignore entirely the needs and interests of fetuses and newborns when setting workplace policies.

Some states, however, have begun to implement legislation that would provide pregnant women with better choices at the workplace. For example, under Connecticut law, it is a

> discriminatory employment practice . . . for an employer, by himself or his agent: . . . (e) to fail or refuse to make a reasonable effort to transfer a pregnant employee to any suitable temporary position which may be available in any case in which an employee gives written notice of her pregnancy to her employer and the employer or pregnant employee reasonably believes that continued employment in the position held by the pregnant employee may cause injury to the employee or fetus.[38]

This law, however, contemplates only one type of accommodation—a temporary transfer to a suitable temporary position. As the Connecticut courts ruled, "[T]he employer need not take any other action to accommodate the employee because the statute, quite simply, does not require it."[39]

One fundamental problem with the equal treatment approach that dominates U.S. case law on the rights of pregnant workers under the PDA is that it forces plaintiffs to engage in an impossible comparison with nonpregnant persons who face similar problems. A case that illustrates this problem is *Troupe v. May Department Stores,*[40] which was cited at the beginning of this chapter and whose opinion was written by Judge Richard Posner. To repeat, the plaintiff, Kimberly Hern Troupe, was employed as a saleswoman in the women's accessories department at Lord & Taylor. Her employment record was "entirely satisfactory" until she became pregnant and began to experience what the court called "morning sickness of unusual severity." Her nausea, however, does not appear to have been limited to the morning. Even when her schedule was adjusted so that she did not need to report to work until noon, she frequently reported late to work or had to leave early. She was fired the day before she was to begin her maternity leave. Citing a statement by her supervisor, Troupe argued that she was fired because her employer did not want to leave her position open during her maternity leave. The lower court granted the defendant's motion for summary judgment, and Troupe appealed. The court of appeals affirmed, concluding that she had failed to sustain a prima facie case of discrimination because "she could not find one nonpregnant employee of Lord & Taylor who had not been fired when about to begin a leave similar in length to hers."

The tone of the *Troupe* opinion is to place all the blame on plaintiff for her problems at work and in litigation. For example, the court explains her "morning sickness" by suggesting that she caused it to last until noon "because she slept later under the new schedule, so that noon was 'morning' for her." Of course, the court does not explain why she also frequently had to leave work early owing to her nausea. Was she napping at the cosmetic counter? As for her inability to provide comparative evidence of discrimination, the court "doubt[s] that finding a comparison group would be that difficult. . . . She either did not look, or did not find." But what was she supposed to find—a nonpregnant employee with a sudden record of tardiness after a nearly spotless work record who also had scheduled a lengthy leave? Other than a pregnant woman, it is hard to imagine a similar subject. Yet Troupe is blamed for not looking, just as she was blamed for having nausea beyond the morning hours. It is also not clear why she should be compared with a "tardy" employee because the record suggests that the plaintiff did offer medical justifications for her lateness. Thus, under the employer's own work rules, Troupe's lateness should have been considered excused rather than unexcused absences.[41]

The tone of the court's opinion is not surprising given Judge Posner's admitted stereotypical views of pregnant women. In a 1989 law review article, he professed the belief that "child-rearing is an area where nature dominates culture" and that sex discrimination is not a likely explanation for women's depressed wages at the workplace.[42] Posner was therefore willing to assume that plaintiff Troupe's "nature" caused her problems at the workplace rather than her employer's discriminatory attitudes.

A sympathetic economic perspective might have asked what business justification an employer could have for dismissing Troupe a day before her pregnancy leave would begin (and her tardiness would certainly end). Since she had a satisfactory work record before becoming pregnant, it is highly likely that she would have returned to work with a satisfactory work record after the completion of her pregnancy leave. If the purpose of punitive action against employees is to correct their behavior, it appears that Lord & Taylor had little cause for concern in Troupe's case. By voluntarily accepting a part-time schedule and making every effort to be on time despite terrible nausea, Troupe demonstrated that she was a devoted employee who could not afford to quit her job. But the Seventh Circuit sympathized entirely with the defendant employer, thereby blaming Troupe for being lazy. The capitalist law and economics orientation of Judge Posner and his associates on the Seventh Circuit apparently made it impossible for them to judge the case from any perspective other than that of the employer. (One must also wonder why an entity that specializes in selling women's clothing would want to hurt its public image by flagrantly mistreating a female employee.)

In fact, however, comparative evidence is not required in all PDA cases; direct evidence of pregnancy-related animus can also prove unlawful discrimination. Had Posner not insisted on an unreasonably narrow interpretation of the PDA, direct evidence of pregnancy animus should have brought the case to the jury (or judge) for ultimate decision under what is termed a *mixed-motives theory*—that an impermissible factor along with an arguably permissible factor motivated her discharge.[43] Instead, the Seventh Circuit never even considered the possibility of a mixed-motives theory, pretending that the PDA permits a finding of liability only through the introduction of comparative evidence.[44]

Although the *Troupe* case is technically a termination case, it can also be seen as a pregnancy leave case. Troupe was doing her utmost to maintain paid employment until the date of her pregnancy leave (when she would most likely not be earning compensation). Her tardiness and early departures from work suggest that paid employment had become extremely difficult for her. Yet she continued to try to work. Why? She probably needed the money, especially anticipating her increased costs and forthcoming leave of absence due to childbirth. The consequence of the discharge was to leave her without a job upon completing her pregnancy leave. In other words, her employer made it impossible for her to combine job security and child care. The price of her decision to take maternity leave after the birth of her child was her employment. If her termination were lawful, even the FMLA would not protect her right to return to work after an unpaid pregnancy leave.

Whereas the Seventh Circuit narrowly construed pregnancy discrimination cases to preclude women from receiving any mandated accommodations during their pregnancy, some Canadian courts have broadly interpreted their own comparable statute to require accommodation. For example, in *Emrick Plastics v. Ontario*,[45] an Ontario court applied a reasonable accommodation model to the case of a pregnant woman who sought reassignment to avoid working in an area where she would be exposed to fumes from spray paint. Applying a disparate impact model, the court concluded that a failure to accommodate pregnant women would effectively exclude the employment of pregnant spray painters and therefore violated the rule against sex discrimination found in the Human Rights Code. The court imposed on the employer the burden of justifying the failure to accommodate as reasonable and bona fide in the circumstances. This result was achieved without relying on any statutory reasonable accommodation language; it was simply an interpretation of settled case law under the Human Rights Code.

Like the PDA, the Ontario Human Rights Act and the Canadian Human Rights Code state that pregnancy-based discrimination is sex discrimination. The Canadian statutes contain no reasonable accommodation requirement for pregnancy or sex discrimination.[46] Yet the courts have implied a resasonable accommodation requirement. The Canadian courts, however, have not been uniformly flexible in providing accommodations that would benefit the fetus or newborn. For example, in *Re Ontario Hydro and Canadian Union of Public Employees, Local 1000*,[47] an arbitration panel refused to grant a man's request for paternity leave following the birth of his second child. He was expected to find paid child care for his children while his wife was incapacitated because of her delivery rather than to provide that care himself.

In case after case in the United States, judges who subscribe to the philosophy of laissez-faire capitalism render narrow decisions in discrimination cases that fail to protect the interests of pregnant women or their newborns. These theorists often opposed the adoption of the PDA and FMLA, and their judicial decisions reflect a total disregard for the substantive protections offered by those statutes.

*Special Treatment Cases.* Even when the PDA was flexibly interpreted to, arguably, accommodate special treatment, it did so under the guise of considering only the needs of the pregnant woman. That is, the facts were distorted to hide the actual benefits to the child. In *California Federal Savings & Loan Association v. Guerra*,[48] the U.S. Supreme Court was faced with whether California's Fair Employment and Housing Act was inconsistent with the PDA[49] by requiring that California employers offer women four months of unpaid disability leave following the birth of a child even if they did not offer disability leave for any other condition. This was dubbed a "special treatment" case because California was requiring that a benefit be provided to (formerly) pregnant women that was not provided to other employees.

The U.S. Supreme Court interpreted the PDA to permit such "special treatment" while also defining the special treatment narrowly to include only the interests of the pregnant woman. "We emphasize the limited nature of the benefits §12945(b)(2) provides. The statute is narrowly drawn to cover only the period of actual physical disability on account of pregnancy, childbirth, or related medical conditions."[50]

The language of the statute and facts of the case, however, are inconsistent with this interpretation of the statute. The statute required up to four months of leave following the birth of a child, which it termed "disability leave." Yet there was no requirement that the woman provide medical certification for this leave. The court of appeal's opinion reflects that Lillian Garland "took a four-month pregnancy disability leave" but contains no evidence that she had a medical reason for four months of leave.[51] Of course, it is possible that she had substantial medical complications following the birth of her child, but it is far more likely that she could not find any suitable alternative child care arrangement for that time period and decided that it was in the best interest of the child for her to stay home and supply that care herself. Interestingly, the Seventh Circuit presumed that women need only ten days to recover from childbirth, whereas the Supreme Court fantasized that it takes women's bodies four months to recover from childbirth. Accordingly, the Supreme Court ignored a likely rationale of the California statute—to facilitate child care in the first four months of a child's life. Thus, the Supreme Court's "special treatment" holding ignored the real beneficiaries of special treatment—the children.

Canadian courts have not been hampered by the special treatment/equal treatment debate. For example, in *Alberta Hospital Association v. Parcels*,[52] the Alberta Court of Queen's Bench was confronted with the question of whether it was discriminatory to deny sick leave benefits to women who were on maternity leave. Sick leave benefits were somewhat more generous than maternity benefits, but as in the *Maganuco* case, employees were not allowed to use maternity and sick leave benefits sequentially. An employee had to choose one or another. Plaintiff Susan Parcels had elected maternity benefits because they were longer in duration but wanted to take advantage of sick leave benefits for that period of her maternity leave in which she was physically incapacitated.

The Alberta court found that Parcels did have a valid claim of sex discrimination because the employer's policy posed a burden to women at the workplace. The employer was not entitled to consider maternity leave as only an example of general non-health-related leave without recognizing its unique health-related aspects. The court ruled that maternity leave "cannot be neatly pigeon-holed because of its hybrid nature. . . . It is a unique situation. As a result, maternity leave should be removed from the leave of absence article in the collective agreement and placed in a category by itself." Rather than adopt a comparative approach, the Alberta court analyzed the situation from the perspective of the well-being of both women and children.

> [T]hose who bear children and benefit society as a whole should not be economically or socially disadvantaged by this activity. . . . [I]t is unfair to impose all of the costs of procreation on one-half of the population. The function of anti-discrimination legislation is to remove this unfair burden from women.

Women will still be the ones who undergo the physical and emotional burdens of pregnancy, but the *Parcels* decisions helps spread those burdens throughout society.

## PROTECTING THE FETUS DURING PREGNANCY

In those cases that have directly raised the issue of the health of fetuses—cases involving reproductive hazards at the workplace—U.S. courts have amazingly managed to decide these cases without really offering any meaningful protection to fetuses. These cases have required the courts to interpret the Occupational Safety and Health Administration (OSHA) or the PDA. In *Oil, Chemical and Atomic Workers International Union v. American Cyanamid Company*,[53] the D.C. Court of Appeals, consisting of Judges Robert Bork, Antonin Scalia, and Stephen Williams, ruled that American Cynamid Company did not violate OSHA by creating a rule that female employees of childbearing age could not hold jobs that exposed them to high levels of lead unless they could show that they had been surgically sterilized. Because surgical sterilization is a medical procedure that can be physically harmful to a woman, OSHA had found that American Cyanamid had violated the general duty clause of the Occupational Safety and Health Act by failing to "furnish employment and a place of employment which were free from recognized hazards that were causing or were likely to cause death or serious physical harm to employees."[54] The D.C. Court of Appeals affirmed the decision of the Occupational Safety and Health Review Commission, which had found that American Cyanamid had not violated OSHA's general duty clause because "an employee's decision to undergo sterilization in order to gain or retain employment grows out of economic and social factors which operate primarily outside the workplace. The employer neither controls nor creates these factors as he creates or controls work processes and materials."

Like the Seventh Circuit's decision in *Maganuco*, the D.C. Circuit held that women's "choices" cannot subject employers to legal liability. Just as the plaintiff Maganuco could have "chosen" to return to work ten days after giving birth without jeopardizing her employment situation, the plaintiffs in *American Cyanamid* could have "chosen" to seek employment elsewhere rather than jeopardize their health through a sterilization operation. Employers are not responsible for the child care problems of a newborn infant or the health consequences of sterilization. As long as women have genuine "choices," we cannot hold employers responsible for the social consequences of their decisions.

Because the *American Cyanamid* decision tolerated the exclusion of women from the workplace as a solution to the problem of reproductive hazards, it set the stage for a PDA challenge to this policy. Amazingly, the Supreme Court managed to decide the PDA case without considering the health interests of the fetus at all. In *International Union v. Johnson Controls*,[55] the Supreme Court ruled that Johnson Controls violated the PDA by excluding from lead-exposed jobs women with childbearing capacity. This result seems appropriate under the U.S. perspective that tries to ignore that pregnant women usually give birth to a child. Federal antidiscrimination law, however, requires us to view the pregnant woman in isolation from the fetus or newborn child. Thus, the Supreme Court can rule that employers may not exclude women from the workplace out of concern for their reproductive health while not providing women with any acceptable, safe options at the workplace. After *Johnson Controls*, a woman must choose between unemployment and working in an environment where she might expose a fetus to harm. The employer is under no obligation to accommodate the needs of women by making the workplace safe. It can simply require her to sign a waiver disclaiming her right to sue if a disabled child is born as a result of reproductive hazards at the workplace.

Other countries have sought to solve the problem of reproductive hazards at the workplace through direct regulation rather than leaving the solution to the private marketplace of coerced consent. In Finland, for example, pregnant workers are entitled to a special, paid maternity leave if the employer cannot ensure that the workplace meets a minimum level of safety for the fetus.[56] The European Union has adopted a directive requiring the removal, but with no reduction in pay, of pregnant or breast-feeding women from positions entailing exposure to fetal health hazards.[57]

The United States' failure to find an acceptable solution to the problem of reproductive hazards at the workplace is symptomatic of its unwillingness to mandate any accommodations for pregnant women in the workplace. The PDA is, at most, an equal treatment model for pregnant women. That is, they must be treated the same as similarly situated, nonpregnant employees. The PDA therefore imposes no duty to accommodate pregnant women if the employer does not have a policy of accommodating other workers with health- or family-related problems. Thus, an employer has no responsibility to excuse a pregnant nurse from treating patients in isolation who might expose the fetus to harm, even when an accommodation could easily be made that would permit the pregnant woman to continue working safely.[58]

In one case involving a pregnant nurse, the plaintiff argued that a failure to modify her work assignments while pregnant would force her to "choose between her job and the health of the fetus."[59] In the name of formal equality, the Eleventh Circuit Court of Appeals found that such a "choice" was consistent with federal antidiscrimination law: "Based on the facts of this case, a pregnant employee, concerned about these increased risks yet still able to continue to work, is faced with a difficult choice. It is precisely this choice, however difficult, that is reserved to the pregnant employee under the PDA and *Johnson Controls*." U.S. law imposes no duty on employers to make workplaces safe for pregnant women while at the same time allowing pregnant women to "choose" to work in environments that pose risks to the fetus. That "choice" is supposed to be a positive expression of our formal equality principle because as the Eleventh Circuit noted, the "[p]laintiff's claims of discrimination are more accurately viewed as an effort to secure preferential treatment for pregnant employees." But of course, it is the fetus, not the pregnant woman, who needs special treatment because it is the fetus, not the pregnant woman, who faces ill health effects from opportunistic infections.

Similarly, in cases in which pregnant women want to perform lighter work in order to avoid a miscarriage, they are primarily concerned about the health of the fetus, not their own health. Federal law offers such women no statutory entitlement to a work environment that is safe for the fetus.[60] Only a society that operates from a laissez-faire economic perspective could fail to systematically protect the well-being of women and children through law.

## Family Medical and Leave Act

### STATUTORY LANGUAGE

The Americans with Disabilities Act was one of the first statutes explicitly to provide accommodations for some employees in private workplaces. Employees who wanted to miss work to receive medical treatment or recover from illness, however, have generally not found the courts receptive to their accommodation requests. If they are repeatedly absent from work, they are not considered to be "qualified" for employment.[61] (By contrast, Canadian courts often find that employees with significant absentee records can still receive the protection of disability discrimination law.)[62] And workers who cannot fit the definition of a "person with a disability," such as pregnant women or workers with temporary medical conditions, cannot make a claim for accommodation under the ADA.[63] Similarly, the Pregnancy Discrimination Amendment to Title VII protects against pregnancy-based discrimination but does not use an affirmative action or reasonable accommodation model for pregnant women. It is modeled entirely on a "formal equality" perspective on discrimination, thereby requiring pregnant women to be treated the same as similarly situated men, whom I have elsewhere called "pregnant men" to emphasize their nonexistence.[64]

Because of the absence of statutory protection for workers who need to miss work because of illness or family-related responsibilities, in the late 1980s Congress began to consider proposals for a federal leave statute. The ultimate outcome of this discussion was the Family and Medical Leave Act of 1993 (FMLA),[65] which gives eligible employees[66] of a covered employer[67] the right to take unpaid leave for a period of up to twelve workweeks in any twelve-month period for one or more of the following reasons:

(A) Because of the birth of a son or daughter of the employee and in order to take care of such son or daughter.
(B) Because of the placement of a son or daughter with the employee for adoption or foster care.

(C) In order to care for the spouse, or a son, daughter, or parent, of the employee, if such spouse, son, daughter, or parent has a serious health condition.

(D) Because of a serious health condition that makes the employee unable to perform the functions of the position of such employee.

The statute defines a "serious health condition" as an "illness, injury, impairment, or physical or mental condition that involves (A) inpatient care in a hospital, hospice, or residential medical care facility; or (B) continuing treatment by a health care provider." Part (A) of the definition is relatively easy to interpret, as it seems to require an overnight stay at a medical institution. Part (B), however, is more ambiguous and has been interpreted through regulations promulgated by the Department of Labor. These regulations specify that a medical condition constitutes "continuing treatment by a health care provider" if it involves

(1) a period of incapacity . . . of more than three consecutive calendar days, and any subsequent treatment or period of incapacity relating to the same condition, that also involves:

(a) treatment two or more times by a health care provider . . . or

(b) treatment by a health care provider on at least one occasion which results in a regimen of continuing treatment under the supervision of the health care provider.

(2) any period of incapacity due to pregnancy, or for prenatal care.

(3) any period of incapacity or treatment for such incapacity due to a chronic serious health condition. A chronic serious health condition is one which:

(a) requires periodic visits for treatment by a health care provider. . . .

(b) continues over an extended period of time . . . and

(c) may cause episodic rather than a continuing period of incapacity. . . .

(4) a period of incapacity which is permanent or long-term due to a condition for which treatment may not be effective. The employee or family member must be under the continuing supervision of, but need not be receiving active treatment by, a health care provider. . . .

(5) any period of absence to receive multiple treatments (including any period of recovery therefrom) by a health care provider . . . either for restorative surgery after an accident or injury, or for a condition that would likely result in a period of incapacity of more than three consecutive calendar days in the absence of medical intervention or treatment.[68]

Although the FMLA was passed despite strong opposition by the business community, it has, in fact, provided little job security for many employees with family or medical leave requests for accommodation. The terms of the statute, coupled with narrow judicial interpretations, have caused this result.

The terms of the statute expressly provide only limited coverage. Only persons who have worked for their employer for at least one year are covered, and only employers with more than fifty employees are covered. Individuals are also excluded if they are among the top 10 percent in salary and benefits compensation at a particular work site. The statute therefore covers only 5 percent of corporations in the United States.[69] And of that 5 percent, only one-third were actually required to make adjustments to be in compliance with the act.[70] And of course, the leave is unpaid, which makes it financially infeasible for many employees. By contrast, European countries, as well as Great Britain and Canada, offer paid leave. For example, the typical European country provides six weeks of paid sick leave, usually at 100 percent of gross earnings.[71] This leave is in addition to paid maternity and parenting leave, as well as unpaid sick leave, usually for up to a year.

Family leave to care for children under the FMLA is limited to the first year of the child's life (or placement with the family) unless the child has a "serious health condition." Thus, a parent who has child care problems after the first year of a child's life can rarely take advantage of the statute's protections. Beyond the child's first year of life, leave is limited to "serious health conditions," which the courts have interpreted as not covering many of the health conditions that cause many parents to miss work to care for their children.

## CASE LAW

*Serious Health Conditions.* The legislature history and regulations concerning the definition of "serious health conditions" suggest that neither Congress nor the Department of Labor has done a good job in constructing a definition that would provide meaningful protection to workers who face job security issues because of health impairments of themselves or their children. The Senate Report, for example, states that

the term "serious health condition" is not intended to cover short-term conditions for which treatment and recovery are very brief. It is expected that such conditions will fall within even the most modest sick leave policies. Conditions or medical procedures that would not normally be covered by the legislation include minor illnesses which last only a few days and surgical procedures which typically do not involve hospitalization and require only a brief recovery period.[72]

The Senate Report then offers examples of such conditions. Many of the examples—"heart attacks, heart conditions requiring heart bypass of valve operations, most cancers, back conditions requiring extensive therapy or surgical procedures, strokes, severe respiratory conditions, spinal injuries"—frequently require far more than twelve weeks of leave from work, especially if the employee has already used up some FMLA leave before selecting a course of treatment for the condition.

The coverage of leave during pregnancy is ambiguous under the FMLA. Obviously, the FMLA covers leave for either parent following the birth of a child, but it is not so clear as to how it treats leave during pregnancy. The Senate Report's list of possible "serious health conditions" includes "ongoing pregnancy, miscarriages, complications or illness related to pregnancy, such as severe morning sickness, the need for prenatal care, childbirth and recovery from childbirth." The regulations promulgated by the Department of Labor, however, do not regard "ongoing pregnancy" as a sufficient basis for medical leave. Instead, the regulations state that there must be a "period of incapacity due to pregnancy, or for prenatal care."[73] The courts have therefore interpreted the FMLA as requiring a woman to have medical proof that her pregnancy is abnormal and incapacitating in order for her to invoke FMLA leave before delivery. Thus, plaintiff Michaela Gudenkauf was found not to be eligible for FMLA protection when she requested part-time work following an episode of contractions in what her physician classified as a normal pregnancy.[74] The medical model underlying the FMLA therefore displays little concern for the normal discomforts of pregnancy, despite its alleged concern for the burdens of pregnancy and childbirth.

The Department of Labor's regulations cover conditions

lasting more than three consecutive calendar days but also state that the regulations ordinarily exclude, "unless complications arise, the common cold, the flu, ear aches." A flu patient may, of course, be sick for a week, and a child with an earache may be home from child care for several days, but both conditions are excluded from the regulations. The regulations do not mention common childhood illnesses such as diarrhea, chicken pox, and "pink eye," which may require exclusion from child care yet not need continuing treatment by a health care provider. The assumption is that employers would not fire parents who have periodic needs to stay home and care for children with common childhood illnesses. The FMLA helps parents staying home with their children during the first year of the child's life (when they can take twelve weeks of leave without demonstrating that the child is ill) but does little for parents when the child is likely to be attending group day care or preschool and is at significant risk of contracting childhood diseases. And when an employee misses work to care for a terminally ill parent, the FMLA covers his or her absence until the parent dies. No leave is available for the time-consuming activities relating to the funeral and estate.[75]

The assumption that employers would not fire parents who miss work to take care of children with common childhood illnesses is not borne out in the case law. For example, OshKosh B'Gosh, a manufacturer of children's clothing, tried to terminate Lilly Crisp after she stayed home with her three-year-old daughter who had had a persistently high fever for several days and had been under a doctor's care during a visit to an emergency room.[76] Crisp was able to prevail in a FMLA challenge, since the medical records demonstrated that the daughter had had a persistent fever for several days and was under a doctor's care, but she was not able to get FMLA protection for sick leave a month earlier when she had flulike symptoms and missed three days of work. Despite a physician's testimony that it would be reasonable to be absent from work for three and one-half days with such an illness (especially since one of the prescribed medications might have affected her ability to operate a sewing machine safely at work), the court found that Crisp had not sustained her burden of proof that she did not work because of a serious health condition. In both instances, the plaintiff faced the same problem—an employer with an inflexible leave policy—but one of her requests for leave fell on the side of statutory protection and the other did not.

Numerous other plaintiffs have lost cases despite being discharged from work because of their own or a family member's medical problems, because they could not meet the "serious health condition" hurdle. Chronic sinusitis bronchitis,[77] a child's ear infection,[78] and food poisoning[79] have been found not to constitute a "serious health condition," although in each case, the employee had little choice but to miss work in response to the health condition. It was not sufficiently serious to evoke statutory coverage, but it was sufficiently serious to cause these people to lose their jobs.

The burden-of-proof rules imposed on the plaintiff in the *OshKosh* case also are insensitive to the realities of the lives of employees who need FMLA protection. The regulations presume that individuals have doctors whom they see for continuing supervision when they have health care problems. In the *Oshkosh* case, for example, the plaintiff's daughter saw a physician at the emergency room of the local hospital for a condition that probably did not require emergency treatment. The plaintiff did see a physician in his office for her earlier illness, but it also appears that she did not have a close personal relationship with the physician. He was able to testify only about what his notes disclosed from the visit; he had no personal memory of it. Because of the vagueness of his notes and recollection, the court found that the plaintiff had not sustained her burden of proof of showing that she had had a serious health condition during her absence from work. Regardless of how sick the plaintiff had been at that time, it is hard to imagine that she could have met her burden of proof unless she visited a hospital emergency room.

Repeated studies have shown that poor people receive inferior medical care, compared with middle-class people, regardless of whether they have health insurance.[80] Furthermore, the FMLA embodies a middle-class expectation for the doctor-patient relationship. But ironically, middle-class persons are likely to have liberal leave policies at work and no need to use the FMLA. Instead, it is working-class employees like Penny Brandon who need to use the FMLA, and they have trouble complying with the medical model that underlies the FMLA.[81] Brandon and other FMLA plaintiffs frequently use hospital emergency rooms for routine medical problems rather than a private physician with whom they have a long-standing relationship.[82] To comply with the FMLA, they are required to make two visits to the doctor for conditions such as chicken pox—for which doctor's visits are usually not encouraged. But if they miss work for more than three days and fail to visit a doctor twice, then they may be denied statutory coverage. Thus, William George prevailed under the FMLA for his six days of leave to recover from chicken pox because he visited both the hospital emergency room and a clinic thereafter, but Audrey Seidle was not able to prevail because her son visited a doctor only one time to be treated for his ear infection.[83] In another case, Christopher Bauer was unable to demonstrate that his rectal bleeding constituted a serious health condition because he missed his second doctor's appointment in order to avoid being absent from work in violation of company policy.[84]

Ironically, it is the United States—which relies primarily on private health care for the treatment of employees—that imposes such stringent certification requirements on employees seeking to take illness-related leave. No parallel rules exist in Canada or European countries where a system of national health insurance also exists. The FMLA primarily covers employers who provide the most minimal benefits at the workplace (most likely not including health insurance) and then asks those employees to document the illnesses—for which they will have to bear the documentation expenses. In other words, the FMLA is premised on a different health delivery model than in fact exists for working-class employees.

It is also extremely difficult for employees to meet the causation standards required under the FMLA to show that their use of their rights under the FMLA motivated a discharge. Applying the rigid burden-of-proof rules developed under Title VII, courts are requiring direct evidence of an illegal motive for an employee to prevail under the FMLA. Circumstantial evidence is insufficient. Thus, Donald Day's evidence that he was discharged on the day that he returned to full-time work following heart surgery was insufficient to prove an illegal discharge under the FMLA.[85] The federal court insisted that in order to prevail, Day should be able to produce "admissible evidence, based on personal knowledge." Employees, however, are unlikely to have stronger evidence than that they were fired as soon as the employer learned they had a serious health condition, since employees are rarely at meetings at which such decisions are made.

Even when defendants concede that the plaintiffs' request triggered their discharge decision, courts have ruled against the plaintiffs under the FMLA. For example, Pat Tuberville was fired two days before she was scheduled for a hysterectomy.[86] In accordance with the FMLA, she had given her employer three weeks' notice of her need for surgery. Her employer then used this notice as an excuse to terminate her, the rationale being that Tuberville was on notice that she would be discharged unless her office improved its work performance. "Since the plaintiff would be on leave the final two weeks of the month and unable to assist in turning the office around," it decided to discharge her when her leave was scheduled to commence. Although the court concluded "that the timing of the leave was a major factor used in making the termination decision," it ruled against the plaintiff because it concluded that she would have nonetheless been eventually discharged. Onerous proof rules can therefore undermine statutory guidelines.

In Europe and Canada, by contrast, these statutory minimums are usually written into the union-employment contract. When Germany tried to cut back its compensation for sick leave, the unions challenged what they perceived to be modifications of the employment contract.[87] Similarly, the unions have responded with widespread strikes when France has tried to cut back on employment rights. But the highly capitalistic structure of the United States means that few workers have guaranteed job rights and that a union's response to cutbacks cannot be anticipated. The employee can use the union to grieve about a failure to follow these rules. Although the union can both educate and advocate for the employee, because of the decline of unionization in the United States, this possibility is relatively rare.

A typical example in Canada that was resolved in the employee's favor was a dispute between Anne French and Bell Canada.[88] French was fired after taking several weeks of sick leave when she was experiencing emotional strain because of her mother's serious illness. Although her emotional strain was apparently heightened by her heavy drinking during this period, the employer did not dispute that her emotional strain caused her to be eligible for illness disability benefits. Rather, her employer criticized French's employment history because she continued to work at her second job during this period and lied when asked if she had a second job. Although Bell Canada policy did not forbid employees from holding second jobs, it did forbid them to claim sick leave on days during which they had worked at another job. French claimed that her emotional distress precluded her from answering telephone calls as an operator for Bell Canada but did not preclude her from working in a solitary position during the day as a mail carrier.

The court's resolution of the case reflects the ways in which Canada's labor law differs from that of the United States. The case is a labor grievance. Thus, French had a union arguing on her behalf (and presumably without compensation). French also had documentation from an apparently sympathetic physician who would have treated her under Canada's national health insurance system. Her family doctor wrote a letter in which he stated that French "has been unable to manage her demanding duties as a Bell operator, although she was still quite capable, in my opinion, of managing her less demanding duties at Canada Post." Rather than a vague recollection, he offered specific, useful information that helped support her claim for disability sick leave. Finally, the standard for "illness" allowed a physician to make fairly vague supporting statements in order for an employee to qualify for sick leave benefits. French's doctor never even gave her condition a name. He just said that "this lady has been under my care" and that "she has been unable to manage her demanding duties." No further documentation of illness was required. Although Bell Canada employed its own physician to monitor sick leave requests, the company physician verified her entitlement to sick leave without examining French and without speaking with her family physician. Ultimately, the plaintiff prevailed in this case because the court did not believe that her conduct had been intentionally fraudulent and thereby could not be a proper basis for discharge. The burden of establishing fraud was placed on the employer, in sharp contrast to U.S. case law, which places all the burdens of proof on the employee. This decision reflects a very different conceptualization of the employer-employee relationship than is embodied in the United States under the FMLA.

*Twelve Weeks.* The FMLA uses one leave period—twelve weeks—which is supposed to be sufficient to protect workers from discharge for all their family and medical leave problems. A woman's pregnancy leave, as well as her family and medical needs, must come out of this twelve-week period. Thus, if she finds it too difficult to work in the last month of her pregnancy, she will have only eight weeks of leave for all her family and medical needs following the delivery of her child. (In addition, she may find that she cannot qualify for any FMLA leave until the baby is born because her pregnancy—despite its many discomforts—is considered to be "normal.") In comparison with European countries, twelve weeks is an extremely stingy number. Nearly every European country provides at least six months of leave for pregnancy alone, with some of that leave permitted before delivery of the baby. Medical leave and parenting leave is in addition to this six months.

Although the FMLA is purportedly geared to providing parents with adequate family leave, it is hard to see how twelve weeks can meet that need in the first year of a child's life. After a woman has taken a minimum of six weeks to recover from her pregnancy, she is left with a maximum of six weeks of parenting and sick leave. The twelve-week figure could be seen as a minimum amount of time to care for the child following its birth before a parent returns to the workplace, but this allows for no absences due to the sickness of the parent or child for the remainder of the year. No European or British country has such an unrealistic expectation of good health in the first year of a child's life.[89] Seventeen of nineteen European or British countries provide for paid sick leave, with most countries not specifying the time period for such leave. Of the countries that specify the length of leave, only one country—Germany—has a limitation equivalent to that of the United States.[90] These countries also offer sick leave in addition to leave for maternity or parenting. The United States, by contrast, specifies a twelve-week period for all forms of leave combined. The U.S. model presumes that most women do and can work until the moment they give birth. We have imposed that rule on our understanding of what is "normal."

The existing twelve-week rule emerged as a legislative compromise in the early stages of the drafting of the FMLA. The original bill, introduced by Congresswoman Patricia Schroeder in 1985, provided for eighteen weeks of unpaid leave over a twenty-four-month period for the birth, adoption, or serious illness of a child, and twenty-six weeks of unpaid leave over twelve-month period for an employee's own serious health condition.[91] In 1987, these time periods were reduced to ten weeks and fifteen weeks, respectively, but the two separate time periods were maintained.[92] Then in 1989 when the bill was reintroduced, the time periods were shortened to ten and thirteen weeks, respectively.[93] Finally, when the first floor vote was taken in the House in 1990, the leaves were combined into one twelve-week leave period per year.[94] This bill was twice passed by the Congress and vetoed by President George Bush[95] before being reintroduced after Clinton was elected president.[96]

The bill that Clinton signed maintained this earlier legislative compromise, with no attempt to return the bill to its more generous and separate time periods. The legislative debate about family and medical leave was therefore shaped at an early stage by the expectation that there would be one combined leave period for both family and medical leave. This is a uniquely American compromise and can be described as a cynical attempt to pass legislation without providing meaningful protection for many American workers. Twelve weeks might be seen as minimally covering the child care obligations immediately following birth but doing little to provide job security to working parents who may have other family or medical leave needs in the year that a child is born. The statute might be named the Family *or* Medical Leave Statute, but it hardly can be characterized as a statute that responds to both a family's dependent care and medical needs.

The testimony offered by child care experts during hearings on the FMLA reflects that twelve weeks is insufficient even for parenting leave, let alone all combined leaves. For example, Dr. T. Berry Brazelton, a world-renowned pediatrician, testified that a newborn needs a minimum of four months of care from a parent in order for appropriate bonding to take place.[97] The Advisory Committee on Infant Care Leave of the Yale Bush Center in Child Development and Social Policy recommended a minimum of six months for parenting leave. Others testified that the standard recommended leave for parents wishing to adopt children is six months.

Despite this testimony, a twelve-week figure for all forms of leave was adopted. In hearings before the Committee on Education and Labor, Congressman William Ford explained why this figure was chosen. The sponsors of the legislation began with a twenty-six-week figure because "that was consistent with what all our trading partners in the Free World do. It was still less than Canada, less than Germany, and less than other major trading partners."[98] He then observed that

> over the years that number was compromised down not because 12 weeks made any more sense to the original sponsors of this legislation than 26, because we could get more people to vote for 12 weeks than we could for 26, including members of this committee who didn't support the bill at the very beginning but began to support the bill after we modified the number of weeks involved.

In other words, the number of weeks chosen had to do with politics, not the needs of the people who would qualify for leave under the FMLA. And the number that was selected was admittedly much lower than the number chosen by our trading partners as well as the number of weeks minimally needed by new parents for the benefit of their children.

*Notice.* When a leave is foreseeable, the FMLA requires that the employee give the employer not less than than thirty days' notice before the date on which the leave is to begin. If the date of the treatment requires the leave to begin in less than thirty days, the employee must provide such notice as is practicable.[99]

Some courts have applied this rule stringently, requiring an employee to invoke the term FMLA when requesting leave, in order to specify statutory coverage. But even the conservative Fifth Circuit Court of Appeals has recognized that this rule departs from Congress's intent. "Congress in enacting the FMLA did not intend employees ... to become conversant with the legal intricacies of the Act."[100] June Manual missed about a month of work following treatment for a health condition and was fired from her job. She challenged her discharge under the FMLA and lost in the trial court. She ultimately prevailed by taking her case to the Fifth Circuit Court of Appeals. It took enormous effort for her to win back the right to work at her blue-collar job, for which she probably received no compensation for her medical leave of absence. And had she not learned of the existence of the FMLA after her discharge, her employer would have gotten away with ignoring its requirements.[101]

Other employees have been less fortunate. Wayne Johnson requested a month's leave without pay because he was "forced by circumstances to [attend to] a matter ... of significant financial importance to [his] immediate and extended family."[102] After his leave request was denied, Johnson was repeatedly absent from work and was ultimately terminated. At his trial, Johnson explained that he needed the time off to monitor his son, who had asthma. The son's grandmother had previously cared for the child when he was ill, but she had recently died. The son had a record of hospitalization for his asthma. Because Johnson had previously received a two-week leave when his son was ill with asthma, the court concluded that "he cannot shield himself behind inexperience or naivete to excuse the alleged drafting error [that is, not mentioning medical condition] for his case differs from that of an inarticulate individual who is disinclined to reveal personal matters such as family illness." Although the FMLA does not require employees to invoke the FMLA by name and does not require notice when leave is unforeseeable, the plaintiff's attempt to foresee his need for leave with a general request for leave was used against him under the statute. Had he made no advance request but found himself requiring emergency days to deal with his son's illness, the court would have had to rule in his favor. His artless attempt to provide notice, however, precluded him from qualifying for FMLA leave.

Notice also works in the other direction. Employers are obligated to inform their employees of their rights under the FMLA. These notice rules are important because many employees are not familiar with the specifics of the FMLA. For example, Lisa Fry, who worked as a head teller for a bank, took sixteen weeks of family leave after the birth of her child.[103] The employee handbook specified that such leave was permitted without the loss of one's employment. Before the FMLA was passed, however, the employer's policy was not to guarantee that an employee be reinstated in his or her prior position. The FMLA, by contrast, states that employees must be reinstated in a comparable position upon their return from covered leave. Thus, the employer would be obligated to comply with the FMLA for those employees who took only twelve weeks of leave but could not be required to comply for those employees who took between twelve and sixteen weeks of leave. Not realizing that the FMLA's rights were limited to twelve weeks of leave, Fry mistakenly thought she would be guaranteed her old position back even if she took sixteen weeks of leave.

Substantively, Fry had no argument under the FMLA that she was entitled to be reinstated in her former position if she took the full sixteen weeks of leave. But procedurally, the court found that her employer was obligated to explain to her the FMLA's consequences of taking more than twelve weeks of leave—that she would not be guaranteed back her old position. In the words of the court:

> We conclude that such claim states a valid cause of action under the FMLA since adequate notice to employees concerning their FMLA right to reinstatement in light of any additional leave permitted by the employer is necessary to enable them to exercise their statutory right to reinstatement by electing to request only twelve weeks of family leave, if the employer's policy so provides.

Lisa Fry is one of the fortunate few to persuade a court to strictly enforce the notice requirements that the FMLA imposes on employers. More often, employees are penalized for their lack of sophisticated knowledge, with little consideration given to how they are supposed to acquire such knowledge. In the absence of a strong union presence in the workplace, it is unrealistic for employees to know much about their rights. Countries like Canada, with a strong union movement, have lower expectations for employees' knowledge than does the United States, where employees' sole source of educational material usually is limited to posters at the workplace.

### Unemployed Parents

U.S. policy has never considered it necessary or appropriate to provide assistance to all parents. When the Aid to Families with

Dependent Children (AFDC) program was instituted in 1935, it was conceived as a temporary measure for widows until they could receive survivor's insurance.[104] Long-term dependence on public assistance was not contemplated. The current trend—in which, on average, half of AFDC recipients receive benefits for seven years—is considered to be politically and socially undesirable. Because long-term dependence on governmental assistance to raise children is considered to be unacceptable, poor mothers are being encouraged (or coerced) to participate in the paid labor force as soon as possible after giving birth to a child. Conservative economists are urging the states to encourage these women to enter the paid labor force six months after the birth of a child or "even before—because it sends the right signal about the importance of responsible behavior."[105] But state support for child care for these women is not necessarily endorsed under the rationale that the "large-scale use of informal arrangements" makes such state sponsorship unnecessary. In other words, there is no reason to guarantee to poor women the same quality of child care arrangements available to middle-class women as we push them from parenting to paid employment.

By contrast, the law of the middle class provides financial assistance until a child reaches the age of eighteen through the dependency deduction in the Federal Income Tax Code. (There is no requirement that both parents be employed in order to receive this deduction.) Moreover, middle-class parents can receive subsidization for child care through their employer's flexible spending plan or through a child care credit on their tax form when both parents are in the paid labor force. The maximum allowance of $6,000 alleviates a substantial portion of most parents' child care costs. Interestingly, this allowance is available only if the parents are using an established child care center or are employing someone who declares his or her earnings to the federal government. "Informal arrangements" are not recognized under this program, even though these informal arrangements are considered sufficient for poor parents.

The recently enacted Personal Responsibility and Work Opportunity Reconciliation Act of 1996 codifies these conservative views. The Reconciliation Act eliminates the entitlement-based Aid to Families with Dependent Children framework and replaces it with a block grant for "temporary assistance for needy families." Foster care and adoption are left as entitlement programs (meaning that all persons are entitled to use those services or programs), but aid to needy families becomes a time-limited and financially limited program. As the statute says, "This part shall not be interpreted to entitle any individual or family to assistance under any State program funded under this part."[106]

This new program is supposed to end "welfare as we know it." To receive the federal money to be disbursed to eligible poor families, a state must prepare a plan that requires "a parent or caretaker receiving assistance under the program to engage in work . . . once the parent or caretaker has received assistance under the program for 24 months (whether or not consecutive)." The states are also required to demonstrate that they have a child support enforcement program as well as a foster care and adoption assistance program, but they are not required to demonstrate that they have an adequate array of child care available for poor families. The only group of poor persons who are partially exempted from these rules are persons who have become impoverished while escaping domestic violence. (Domestic violence is narrowly defined as being "battered or subjected to extreme cruelty.") They apparently are considered to be the "deserving poor," compared with nonbattered women who merely find it difficult to combine parenting and paid employment.

The Reconciliation Act also offers to the states some interesting financial incentives. States are entitled to receive a "bonus" for each year in which they demonstrate a net decrease in out-of-wedlock births while also demonstrating a lower rate of induced pregnancy terminations. (This rule seems premised on the inaccurate stereotype that women on welfare have, on average, more children than do other women. It also suggests that they should not use a lawful means of preventing childbirth and should get married, regardless of the quality of their marital relationship.)

Although most married women who have paid employment while raising young children work on a part-time basis, the Reconciliation Act incorporates a model of nearly full-time employment. For the purpose of defining whether a recipient "is engaged in work," the goal by the year 2000 is for the parent in a single-parent family to be working at least thirty hours per week. Even if a woman is fortunate enough to have a job that parallels the hours of a school day and to have children who are old enough to attend school, it is impossible to work thirty hours per week and be home when children leave for school and arrive home at the end of the day. Of course, the states are not required to create after-school or before-school programs for parents whose workday does not perfectly match the school day. (There is a modest exception for a single parent with a child under the age of six: in that case, the work requirement is lowered to twenty hours per week.)

One has to wonder what kind of work Congress expected parents of young children would be able to find that would make it possible for them to afford the necessary child care and other expenses of employment. Congress does, however, define "work," thus giving us some insight into their thinking. One activity that counts as "work" is "the provision of child care services to an individual who is participating in a community services program." Women are required to leave their children at home to take care of the children of other women who are engaging in low-paying community service work. This rule is comparable to the general exclusion of domestic workers from minimum wage laws. When the government interferes in the economy, it always tries to ensure that it does not eliminate a source of low-paid domestic labor.

The public rhetoric on behalf of the Reconciliation Act is that U.S. policy needs to change the cultural attitudes of the poor so that we can break the cycle of poverty. Forcing families with young children off public assistance within two years is supposed to promote an appropriate work ethic. Nowhere in this discussion does there appear to be concern for the quality of life that we will be creating for children. Whereas middle-class mothers are made to feel guilty if they place too high a priority on work, poor mothers are told to find paid employment even if it is detrimental to the well-being of their children.

But the policies underlying the new welfare law do not simply consist of withdrawing from poor people public support for parenting. The policies also push a moralistic agenda that these women should get married, have fewer children, and not have abortions. (In addition, the child support enforcement rules require mothers to divulge the paternity of the father of their child, regardless of whether he could support the child financially.) As in the gay rights area, we see a combination of capitalism and moralism that is functionally unnecessary to capitalism.

Amazingly, even capitalists would have trouble justifying these new rules in the name of economic efficiency. It is openly predicted that these rules will create greater use of the foster care and adoption systems—both of which are far more expensive than welfare. And given the evidence of the questionable quality of the foster care and adoption systems, there is little reason to believe that these expensive changes would benefit children. Children in middle-class families will benefit from the family law presumption that it is in their best interest to live with and be raised by their biological parents. But children in poor families are openly penalized for their parents' poverty—they either become poorer or participate in foster care drift. Neither result is exactly in their best interest despite the "profamily" rhetoric.

No other Western nation tries to instill work-ethic values in parents by penalizing their children. No other country makes such a sharp distinction between the rights of poor children and the rights of middle-class children. Other countries offer benefits to all parents and then try to help the transition to work by providing child care and universal health insurance. The result is a lower rate of labor market participation by mothers in the early years of a child's life but a higher rate of labor market participation in later years.

France, for example, has a more generous financial assistance program for single parents with young children[107] than does the United States, and the employment rate for single parents with children under age three is lower in France than in the United States (43 percent versus 50 percent). But the employment rate of single parents with children aged three to five is higher (66 percent versus 61 percent) in France than in the United States. Current American welfare law presumes that more than two years of dependence on public assistance fosters long-term unemployment among single parents, but the French experience shows that single parents can be helped, with great success, to return to work after three years of public assistance. The beneficiaries are the children as well as the mothers who do not face an impossible balancing act between work and home. When feminists note, as they have in Sweden, that women are the ones who are disproportionately leaving the workforce to care for children, the response is to try to increase the incentives to get men to stay home with the children rather than to get more women back into the labor market more quickly.[108]

America's version of hypercapitalism has caused it to avoid governmental intervention on behalf of parents. Thus, we have little guaranteed leave for working parents and a limited scheme of benefits for nonworking parents that is shrinking further. These results may be consistent with a laissez-faire attitude toward labor market intervention but are not consistent with the best interests of the children or their parents. By assuming that parents who receive public financial assistance inevitably have a poor work ethic, U.S. policy has consistently failed to offer positive incentives to parents of older children to get them into the paid workforce. But the experience of other countries suggests that such policies are possible and are more effective than the punitive approach currently embodied in the new welfare law.

In the United States, it is virtually unthinkable that we would mandate paid leave for pregnant women and their partners, require accommodations during pregnancy, and insist on the availability of pregnancy-related insurance benefits for all women. Yet these kinds of benefits and more are routine in Canada and western Europe. The basic style of discourse in discussing these pregnancy-related issues in the United States is unique. U.S. law regarding pregnancy and childbirth reflects the tenets of laissez-faire economics—that we should solely consider the autonomy rights of corporations or adults in our society when deciding whether to mandate benefits.

In Canada and western Europe, by contrast, the starting premise is quite different. The needs of children both before and after birth are at the center of the discussion, although the equality rights of women and men in society are also emphasized. This focus on children, without the expectation that we will pass on all the costs of childbearing and childrearing to women and their partners, results in an entirely different set of social policies than we see in the United States. Workplace accommodations during and after pregnancy become possible not as special treatment for women but as special treatment for fetuses and newborns. Adhering to a strict capitalist philosophy, the United States is not simply passing on the costs of pregnancy and childbirth to parents, especially female parents, but is endangering the welfare of our children.

My point is not that we should ignore the equality interests of adult women and men but that we should also work harder to incorporate the needs of children into those equality rights. Parenting leave is not simply giving women a chance to recover from the physical demands of pregnancy and childbirth but is also facilitating the care of children following birth. Accommodating pregnant women at the workplace is not simply protecting their right to work while pregnant but is also creating a workplace that is safe for fetuses. Canada and western Europe have managed to find solutions that protect the interests of children as well as female employees. But this conversation has not even begun in the United States.

# 5

## SEXUAL ORIENTATION DISCRIMINATION

When Perry Watkins, an African American gay man, was drafted by the U.S. Army in 1967 during the Vietnam conflict, he had no idea that he would eventually have to bring a lawsuit to retain a position in the armed forces.[1] Despite indicating on his preinduction physical form that he had "homosexual tendencies," he was found qualified for admission and inducted into the armed forces. A year after entering the army, Watkins sought discharge by again stating that he had "homosexual tendencies" and had even committed "sodomy" with other members of the military. After a brief investigation, the army found him qualified to be retained. In 1975, however, although the army attempted to discharge Watkins based on his sexual orientation, a review board concluded that "there is no evidence suggesting that his behavior has had either a degrading effect upon unit performance, morale or discipline, or upon his own job performance."[2]

At first, Watkins's race seems to have caused the army to overlook his sexual orientation: "Every *white* person I knew from Tacoma who was gay and had checked [the homosexuality] box 'Yes' did not have to go into the service. They were called in and asked, 'What does this mean?' They said, 'It means I'm gay. I like to suck dick.' 'Fine, You can go.'"[3] Similarly, in 1968, Watkins observes: "There was another person who went to his commander and told him the same damn thing and they let him go home. Of course, he was white. Which I think also had something to do with it—he was white and I was black."

The army's policy of overlooking Watkins's homosexuality, however, changed in 1981 as the cold war began to wind down. Although Watkins now wanted to stay in the military, which he regarded as his career, the army commenced discharge proceedings against him based entirely on evidence that had been available to it at the 1968 and 1975 discharge proceedings. This time, the review board decided that Watkins was not fit for service and should be discharged.[4] His sexual orientation became a more dominant concern of the army as its need for military personnel declined. An openly gay African American soldier was no longer acceptable, regardless of his service record.

Watkins's 1982 discharge became the subject of a lengthy court proceeding that was not resolved until 1989. His legal battle is well known in the gay and lesbian community because Watkins is one of a few gay plaintiffs to prevail in a federal legal proceeding. What is distinctive about Watkins's case is the persistent attempt by the courts to fashion a victory for him without creating legal advances for gay men and lesbians in the military or elsewhere.

Watkins prevailed on "estoppel" and "double jeopardy"[5] grounds, but not because the military's treatment of gay men was unconstitutional. (The original Ninth Circuit opinion that decided his case on the merits was ultimately vacated by an en banc panel of the Ninth Circuit.)

When Michael Hardwick was arrested for drinking in public as he left his employment at a gay bar in Atlanta, he had no idea that this same police officer would later arrest him in his own bedroom for a sodomy violation.[6] But in a complicated twist of errors—a mistake on a hearing notice, an expired warrant for his arrest, and a sleepy friend in the living room who mistakenly directed a police officer to his bedroom—Michael Hardwick became the plaintiff in a landmark civil rights lawsuit to challenge Georgia's sodomy law. Hardwick's "crime" was engaging in mutual oral sex with another man in his own bedroom. His "crime" made him subject to arrest because he was openly identifiable as a gay man through his employment at a gay bar. Had Michael Hardwick been employed in a less "ghettoized" setting and resided in a more private situation, he would not have been arrested for engaging in mutual oral sex. Whereas Watkins's legal problems began when as an African American man, he found himself coercively subjected to the draft, Hardwick's legal problems began when as a working-class man, he found himself a victim of police harassment. In both cases, these men were vulnerable to the state's coercion because they were a particularly disadvantaged subclass of the gay and lesbian community.

When W, an Australian lesbian, had two children as a result of artificial insemination in the late 1980s when living with her partner, G, she, too, had no idea that she would become a well-known figure in the gay and lesbian community because of her legal battles.[7] Like Watkins and Hardwick, W was not a highly privileged member of society. Aside from a position as a kennel hand and counter clerk, she had been mostly unemployed since the mid-1980s. G, too, had minimal income until her father died in 1994, leaving her a substantial estate. When W and G separated in 1994, G refused to assist financially in the raising of the children that had been borne to W with G's alleged encouragement. In the first decision of its kind in a common law legal system, the Supreme Court of New South Wales ordered G to provide a lump sum payment to be used to purchase annuities to help support the children.[8] W, a working-class lesbian who found herself in financial distress, was able to obtain relief through legal proceedings in Australia.

Similarly, gay men and lesbians have been able increasingly to use the Canadian legal system to gain relief in cases involving their family and employment situations. In 1992, the Canadian Federal Court found that a discharge from the military following an admission of homosexuality violated the plaintiff's equality rights under the Canadian Charter of Rights and Freedoms.[9] In *Haig v. Canada*,[10] the Ontario Court of Appeal concluded that it was discriminatory for the Canadian Human Rights Act to omit "sexual orientation" from its list of grounds of unlawful discrimination. Applying that rule, it concluded that it was unlawful for a captain in the Canadian armed forces to be denied eligibility for promotion and career training when he revealed that he was a homosexual.

U.S. Supreme Court precedent, as enunciated in *Bowers v. Hardwick*,[11] has left gay men and lesbians outside constitutional protection. Judges like Ninth Circuit Judge Stephen Reinhardt have found themselves bound by *Bowers* and therefore unable to rule on behalf of homosexual plaintiffs. Reinhardt dissented from the decision in *Watkins II* while acknowledging that "homosexuals have been unfairly treated both historically and in the United States today" and that "proper interpretation of constitutional principles" would give them constitutional protection.[12] Nonetheless, he felt bound by the Supreme Court's 1986 decision in *Bowers*, which leaves homosexuals outside constitutional protection. Reinhardt's dissent acknowledges the obvious—that equality principles do not extend to constitutional decision making when the plaintiffs are gay men or lesbians in the United States.

A close examination of gay rights litigation in the United States reveals the twin themes of militarism and moralism that underlie American-style capitalism. Militarism has a complicated relationship to American capitalism, and the disproportionate subsidization of the military has a long-standing history in American politics. During the New Deal era, America briefly experimented with becoming a social welfare state in which all workers could be guaranteed minimum wages and benefits. Following World War II, however, the social welfare policies became minimal except for veterans.

> Hence the war brought what the New Deal reformers had hoped to avoid: a special welfare state for a substantial sector of the population deemed especially deserving. The social reformism of the New Deal had been channeled into expanded public provision for veterans, making it henceforth less likely that establishment of a national welfare state could be completed.[13]

Even today, with the end of the cold war, the Republican Congress has resisted attempts to close bases and radically limit military spending. By contrast, Great Britain enacted sweeping social reforms during this same period, which were available to all members of society, not just veterans. The United States has continued to expand its subsidization of the military while largely abandoning its New Deal aspirations of a social welfare state. "[T]he New Deal dream of national social and economic policies to meet the many needs of all Americans had been dissolved by the domestic politics of the war years. The dream would not soon reappear, and never again in the same way."[14]

In more recent times, while the Republican Congress has attempted to end government-sanctioned support of industry by eliminating the Department of Commerce, it has also insisted on approving more money for military spending than proposed by the Clinton administration. Laissez-faire Republicans have not been willing to acknowledge the lessened need for military spending at the end of the cold war. Newt Gingrich, for example, has insisted that the world is full of "clever countries" that are trying to "learn how to cope with an American military force."[15] But his real reason to support outmoded and unneeded military technology in the post-cold war era is to keep the B-2 contractors in business. Thus, although a large military-industrial complex may be historically understood as a response to Communism, it currently has a life of its own. And that life contradicts the laissez-faire principles of capitalism by standing as the most subsidized segment of the American economy.

The treatment of gays in the military, however, cannot be explained solely by American deference to the military's stated needs. After all, excluding individuals like Watkins deprives the military of highly qualified personnel and makes little sense in a country devoted to a powerful military. To explain the adverse treatment of gays in the military, we thus need to refer to the

moralism underlying American-style capitalism. House majority leader (Republican) Dick Armey argues that democracy and
capitalism derive from a higher power.[16] Irving Kristol, the
father of neoconservatism, claims that any attack on religion is
an attack on capitalism, a moralistic perspective that has prevented the United States from opening the doors of privilege to
all its members.

Legal moralism in the United States has not been limited to
claims involving military service. When gay men and lesbians
tried to use the legal system's promise of gender equality to
have marriage extended to them on the same basis as heterosexuals, the *Wall Street Journal* published an editorial criticizing the court's intervention in a matter that should be decided
by the people.[17] As a proponent of laissez-faire capitalism, the
*Wall Street Journal* should, for consistency's sake, have published an article describing the economic inefficiency of allowing some members of our society, but not others, to take advantage of the economic advantages of marriage. Capitalists pretend
that extending benefits to gay men and lesbians constitutes
"special protection" rather than formal equality, so as to avoid
applying laissez-faire principles to gay men and lesbians.

Legal academics suffer from the same blind spot. Richard
Posner's willingness to accede to moralistic arguments is apparent in his book *Sex and Reason*. In discussing the gay marriage
issue, Posner acknowledges that "authorizing homosexual marriage would have many collateral effects, simply because marriage is a status rich in entitlements."[18] After recognizing that
granting these benefits to gay men and lesbians would have
moral and political implications, he concludes: "These questions
ought to be faced one by one rather than elided by conferring all
the rights of marriage in a lump on homosexuals willing to

undergo a wedding ceremony." Laissez-faire principles were abandoned in the name of deferring to moralism when the rights of gay and lesbian people were at stake.

Capitalism and homophobia do not have an inherent functional relationship. Capitalism is based on laissez-faire principles that seek to attain economic efficiency by allowing each person in society to realize his or her potential without interference by the state. But American law is not evenhanded when it considers the rights of gay and lesbian people in comparison to heterosexuals. Indeed, American capitalism is a peculiarly moralistic and militaristic version of capitalism. Rather than make moral arguments, such as gay people deserve to be treated worse than others, American capitalists often hide their moral disgust with special treatment arguments.

There is one seeming contradiction in this account—*Romer v. Evans*—the Colorado ballot initiative case in which the U.S. Supreme Court concluded that animus against homosexuals was not a legitimate basis for denying them legal rights. Nonetheless, as we will see, this case is consistent with American-style laissez-faire capitalism because it refuses to recognize the historical mistreatment of gay men and lesbians and renders its decision in a way that upholds the anti-affirmative action bias of American law. Its decision leaves in place the moralism and militarism underlying American law.

## Constitutional Law

### THE BAD NEWS

It should not surprise us that Michael Hardwick, the gay bartender, lost his constitutional claim to privacy under the American Constitution in *Bowers v. Hardwick*.[19] Not able to afford to purchase privacy in his life, he could not expect the courts to give him constitutional protection. Although a strict application of laissez-faire principles should prevent the government from interfering with the private sexual practices of gay men and lesbians—just as it does not interfere with the private sexual practices of middle-class heterosexuals[20]—the Court refused to extend these principles to gays and lesbians. The state's justification for its sodomy law in *Bowers* was the "belief of a majority of the electorate in Georgia that homosexual sodomy is immoral and unacceptable." The Supreme Court concluded that this justification was sufficient to uphold a law that infringes on the private sexual activity of adults.

As Chief Justice Warren Burger stated in his concurrence in *Bowers*: "To hold that the act of homosexual sodomy is somehow protected as a fundamental right would be to cast aside millennia of moral teaching." The Court therefore refused to extend to homosexuals the laissez-faire doctrine of privacy as developed in the contraception and abortion cases. As the dissent noted, "The legitimacy of secular legislation depends . . . on whether the State can advance some justification for its law beyond its conformity to religious doctrine. . . . A State can no more punish private behavior because of religious intolerance than it can punish such behavior because of racial animus." The dissent's argument would be valid if gay men and lesbians received constitutional protection. But because their claims lie outside constitutional protection, moral arguments are allowed to justify infringement on their liberty interests.

Similarly, the courts have continuously denied claims by gay men and lesbians that they should be entitled to enter military service on the same basis as do heterosexuals. In the cases brought under equality doctrine (unlike *Watkins*), the plaintiffs have consistently lost. The Fourth Circuit Court of Appeals, for example, accepted the argument that "sexual tensions and attractions could play havoc with a military unit's discipline and solidarity."[21] Relying on the precedent of *Bowers*, the court also noted, "Given it is legitimate for Congress to proscribe homosexual acts, it is also legitimate for the government to seek to forestall these same dangers by trying to prevent the commission of such acts." As the dissent observes, these kinds of arguments used to support white male supremacy. "`Unit cohesion' is a facile way for the ins to put a patina of rationality on their efforts to exclude the outs. The concept has therefore been a favorite of those who, through the years, have resisted the irresistible erosion of white male domination of the armed forces." The U.S. Constitution, however, has not yet been interpreted to protect gay men and lesbians from the forces of "white male domination." Free-speech arguments under the First Amendment have also been unavailable to gay men and lesbians in the military, despite the explicit silencing of speech intended by the current "don't ask, don't tell" policy.[22]

Until recently, the Canadian courts also refused to allow gay men and lesbians to receive constitutional protection. In 1993, the Ontario court (General Division) ruled in a two-to-one decision that it did not violate the equality provision in the Charter of Rights for two men to be denied the right to seek a marriage license.[23] In a curious turn of logic, the court found that there was no sexual orientation discrimination because the marriage law does not prohibit gay people from marrying, it only prohibits them from marrying someone of the same sex. (The argument does not appear to have been made that the rule constituted sex discrimination.) A month earlier in 1993, the Supreme Court of Canada concluded that it did not constitute unlawful "family status" discrimination for a man to be denied bereavement leave to attend the funeral of the father of his same-sex partner, although the court clearly left open the question whether such a rule would constitute sexual orientation discrimination.[24] In a stinging dissent, Justice Claire L'Heureux-Dubé surveyed the literature on the structure of the urban black family in the United States and argued, "While the structure of the family may be a question of choice for some, for others the structure of family may be in part a natural response to social and political pressures." She saw the connection between economics and family structure and did not presume that the state should use its power to coerce people into conventional family arrangements in order to make claims for benefits.

In 1995, the Supreme Court of Canada ruled in *Egan v. The Queen*,[25] that the infringement of equality was justifiable in a case involving the federal old-age security legislation. This legislation provides an allowance to the spouse of a pensioner, with a spouse defined as a person of the opposite sex. Although the court found that this definition did violate the right to equality as guaranteed by Section 15 of the Charter, the court also found that such discrimination was constitutional under Section 1 of the Charter. The majority acknowledged that the purpose of the rule was to support the "heterosexual family unit." "It is the social unit that uniquely has the capacity to procreate children and generally cares for their upbringing, and as such warrants support by Parliament to meet its needs. . . . [T]his is the unit in society that fundamentally anchors other social relationships and other aspects of society." Like the cases in the United States, this case merged moralism with laissez-faire capitalism. Although as acknowledged by the court, the general rule was to extend benefits without regard to sexual orientation, the court allowed the government to violate that rule in order to benefit the traditional, heterosexual family unit composed of a wage earner, dependent spouse, and children.

Nonetheless, in the last several years in Canada, using constitutional litigation, there have been many successful attempts to secure same-sex partner supplemental health care benefits. One of the first successful challenges came from the province of Manitoba. Since 1973, Chris Vogel had been a regular full-time employee of the government of Manitoba.[26] In 1974, he participated in a marriage ceremony conducted by the Unitarian Church, but because his partner was of the same sex, the registrar of vital statistics refused to register the marriage. Some of his employment benefits included benefits to his "spouse," such as dental insurance, a semiprivate hospital plan, an extended health plan, and various pension and survivor's benefits. The Manitoba court concluded that the exclusion of homosexual partners from the employee benefits program constituted discrimination on the basis of sexual orientation and referred the case back to the human rights adjudicator for a decision. Recognizing that it might be difficult for the legislature to change the law, the Manitoba court admitted, "We can't say we are too busy with other things or that the issue is too politically sensitive or set up a Royal Commission. We do our duty and decide." Rather than duck the issue, the court applied traditional principles of equality doctrine to conclude that sexual orientation discrimination underlay the employee benefit program.

Similarly, in *M. v. H.*,[27] the Ontario trial court concluded in 1996 that it was unconstitutional for the spousal support legislation to exclude same-sex couples from coverage. In this case, it was clear that the courts achieved a result that was not possible in the legislature. In 1993, the Ontario Law Reform Commission recommended that same-sex couples receive some legislative recognition. In 1994, the Equality Rights Statute Amendment Act, bill 167, was put forward in the Ontario legislature. The bill was defeated and has not been reintroduced. Furthermore, the government's actions with respect to this litigation show how hard it is to achieve governmental consensus on this issue. Initially, the attorney general intervened in this case and supported the plaintiff's case. Then after the election of 1995, the attorney general filed another brief in support of the defendant. As the court found, "It is simply not realistic to regard the current state of Ontario law pertaining to spousal support as merely part of a process of legislative reform." After considering various arguments for judicial deference, the court decided to move forward and grant relief to the plaintiff.

In more recent cases, the Canadian courts have been increasingly willing to accord same-sex couples the family rights of married partners, by examining the cases as sexual orientation cases. In a 1995 decision, *Re Metro Toronto Reference Library and C.U.P.E., Loc. 1582*,[28] the arbitrator resolved the issue left open by *Mossop*—whether a denial of bereavement leave to a same-sex partner constituted sexual orientation discrimination. The arbitrator answered this question in the affirmative. While U.S. courts have consistently refused to recognize the inappropriateness of discrimination on the basis of sexual orientation, Canadian courts have increasingly recognized the history of prejudice and hatred against gay and lesbian people. Rather than try to twist gay rights arguments into gender arguments, they deal with them directly as arguments based on the inappropriateness of sexual orientation discrimination. They are not afraid to confront directly the moral arguments supporting sexual orientation discrimination.

Despite some early losses in arbitration cases,[29] the current trend is also to extend rights to same-sex couples in that judicial arena. In *Re Bell Canada and Canadian Telephone Employees' Association*,[30] the arbitrator ruled that spousal benefits must be accorded to same-sex couples in order to comply with the Canadian Human Rights Act. Those benefits included a pension plan, survivor protection benefits, and various health care benefits beyond those offered automatically by the government. The arbitrator concluded that there had been unlawful discrimination on the basis of sexual orientation. Likewise, in *Re Treasury Board (Environment Canada) and Lorenzen*,[31] the arbitrator concluded that an employer violated the collective-bargaining agreement and the Canadian Human Rights Act by not allowing bereavement and family leave to be accorded to a same-sex partner. The arbitrator did not have to reach the Human Rights Act issue because he concluded that as used in the collective-bargaining agreement, the term *spouse* could include same-sex couples. In the absence of the terms *husband* and *wife*, he concluded that such an interpretation was reasonable.

Although Australian courts have not gone so far as to decide that same-sex relationships should be directly recognized as marriages, they have extended the benefits of the law of marriage to same-sex couples in divorcelike proceedings. An example is the previously cited *W v. G* case,[32] the female plaintiff who sued her female partner for child support under an equitable estoppel theory, with the Supreme Court of New South Wales ruling in favor of the plaintiff.

The Australian decision is, in many respects, a classic example of laissez-faire decision making. The sexual orientation of the parties played no role in the decision. The court simply applied long-standing equitable principles to a case involving a same-sex couple. Moralistic arguments did not influence the judgment, thereby allowing the court to extend the protection of the law in an evenhanded manner. No court in the United States has been willing to apply such equitable principles to cases involving children raised by same-sex couples. The Australian decision is therefore remarkable for what it does *not* do: It does not apply moral blinders to prevent same-sex couples from receiving the benefits of the law.

But the New South Wales decision also has limited implications. This is not a case in which an intact same-sex couple is trying to take advantage of benefits accorded to heterosexual couples, such as health insurance and tax benefits. Instead, this is a case in which one member of a relationship has a claim against another member. Thus a victory for the lesbian plaintiff is a loss for the lesbian defendant. The court has therefore allowed standard legal principles to govern the income redistribution as between two lesbians. It would be a far more radical step for the court to allow a same-sex couple to take advantage of general societal benefits that are exclusively reserved for heterosexuals. Then the gay or lesbian plaintiffs would be making a claim against the resources of society in general, rather than against the resources of the members of their own community.

## THE GOOD NEWS

The decision by the Hawaii Supreme Court to apply equality doctrine to a marriage claim by a same-sex couple has been heralded as a great victory in the gay and lesbian community. But the Hawaii court couched its decision in gender rather than sexual orientation terms and therefore did not have to confront directly the moral arguments used in the United States to justify sexual orientation discrimination. In *Baehr v. Lewin,*[33] the

Hawaii Supreme Court ruled that the Hawaii marriage statute presumptively constituted unconstitutional discrimination based on sex. The court's decision completely ignored the petitioners' sexual orientation; in fact, it was not even considered to be relevant to the Court's decision. Observing simply that an individual could marry a man only if she were a woman, the court concluded that the marriage rule constituted a sex-based rule. The fact that the historical origins of such a rule reflected animus on the basis of sexual orientation rather than gender was not relevant to the court's decision. Its decision reflected an analysis of the language, rather than the intent or history, of the challenged statute. By employing such an analysis, the court was able to rule for the petitioners without reaching the thorny question of whether discrimination on the basis of sexual orientation should be tolerated.

In 1996, the U.S. Supreme Court handed gay rights activists their first major victory before the highest court in a six-to-three decision in *Romer v. Evans*.[34] The Court held that the voters of the state of Colorado acted unconstitutionally when they approved an amendment to their state constitution that would prohibit all legislative, executive, or judicial actions designed to protect the rights of any gay, lesbian, or bisexual person on the basis of his or her sexual orientation. Although gay rights activists have heralded *Romer v. Evans* as "a landmark civil-rights ruling,"[35] the Supreme Court's decision in that case is actually consistent with its trend toward accepting the principles of formal equality and avoiding moral issues in gay rights cases. This case can be understood as consistent with the anti-affirmative action backlash described in previous chapters. It may reflect a short-term victory for gay and lesbian people, but it also reflects a long-term trend toward undermining affirmative action. It also says nothing about overturning *Bowers v. Hardwick*, therefore still leaving gay men and lesbians without constitutional protection.

The *Wall Street Journal* has grasped this connection. In an editorial following the *Romer* decision, the *Journal* said that it was "cheered" to see Justice Anthony Kennedy recite the famous line from *Plessy v. Ferguson* that the Constitution "neither knows nor tolerates classes among citizens"[36] because that statement clarifies that the Court "is starting to make color-blindness a reality."[37] As the *Journal* noted, the doctrine underlying *Romer* better reflects the anti-affirmative action backlash than a positive statement about the rights of gay and lesbian people. The author of the Court's opinion, Justice Kennedy, applied the formal equality principles that he had previously applied to reverse discrimination cases in order to overturn the Colorado amendment. The doctrine that he applied was not novel; what was novel was his willingness to extend that doctrine to a case that involved gay and lesbian petitioners.

The surprising result for someone who expects the Court to follow principles of formal equality and laissez-faire capitalism in an evenhanded manner is that Justices Antonin Scalia, William Rehnquist, and Clarence Thomas filed strong dissents. Despite their stance as the strongest proponents of formal equality doctrine on the Court, they could not leave aside their moralistic impulses to extend those principles to gay men, lesbians, and bisexuals. They had to lump the case into the "special treatment" category in order to rationalize the failure to apply principles of formal equality to gay and lesbian petitioners.

"The amendment prohibits special treatment of homosexuals, and nothing more,"[38] argued Justice Scalia in vigorously dissenting from the majority's holding. "The principle," he contended, that underlies the majority's opinion

> is that one who is accorded equal treatment under the laws, but cannot as readily as others obtain preferential treatment under the laws, has been denied equal protection of the laws. If merely stating this alleged "equal protection" violation does not suffice to refute it, our constitutional jurisprudence has achieved terminal silliness.

Scalia, whose opinions are usually known for their close reading of the text, must ignore completely the language of the challenged amendment to arrive at that conclusion. It is true that the amendment would prohibit special treatment on behalf of gay, lesbian, and bisexual people, since it prohibits any "quota preferences" for such groups. But it is also true that the amendment prohibits antidiscrimination protection as well. It clearly states that branches of government may not "enact, adopt or enforce any statute, regulation, ordinance or policy whereby homosexual, lesbian or bisexual orientation, conduct, practices or relationships shall constitute or otherwise be the basis of or entitle any person or class of persons to have . . . claim of discrimination." As the majority stated, the result of the adoption of the amendment would be to invalidate nondiscrimination ordinances passed by the cities of Denver and Boulder. It took no grand constitutional analysis to apply the plain language of the amendment to the plain language of the local ordinances. In fact, although Scalia accuses the majority of "terminal silliness," he offers no alternative interpretation of the amendment as applied to the Boulder and Denver ordinances. Nondiscrimination can no longer be offered to gay, lesbian, and bisexual people after the adoption of Amendment 2. It is this nondiscrimination principle that Justice Kennedy's opinion claimed must be protected by the Equal Protection clause, no more and no less.

Scalia sets up the case as a special protection case so that he does not have to distinguish it from the long line of formal equality cases that he has followed so passionately. The legal question that he sees as underlying this case is "whether there was a legitimate rational basis for the substance of the constitutional amendment—for the prohibition of special protection for homosexuals." He then chides the majority for avoiding discussion of this question, "since the answer is so obviously yes." Scalia is correct that virtually no group, and certainly not a group composed of gay men and lesbians, can make a constitutional claim for special protection under existing jurisprudence. The majority fails to ask that question because it is irrelevant to the case before the Court. Amendment 2 is unconstitutional under existing doctrine not because it prohibits special treatment for gay men and lesbians but because it also invalidates laws that promise equal treatment. Scalia fails to explain why gay men and lesbians are not "persons" who, like white heterosexual men, are entitled to the equal protection of the laws as guaranteed by the Fourteenth Amendment.

The majority and dissenting opinions in *Romer* are ships passing in the night because they ask and answer entirely different questions. Jurisprudentially, however, they actually seem to agree on a core principle—that gay men and lesbians are not entitled to special protection. Both the majority and minority opinions are premised on a commitment to formal equality. The dissent is forced to distort the plain meaning of the amendment to take it out of formal equality doctrine.

The dissent distorts the amendment's language to placate the moralism of Colorado voters. Even Scalia has to admit that the

Colorado voters were trying to "preserve traditional sexual mores" through the passage of Amendment 2 although he also tries to hide their moralism by describing them as "seemingly tolerant."

Had Scalia been truly committed to the values of laissez-faire capitalism, rather than the values of the so-called moral majority, he would have had to note the inefficiency of allowing the Colorado voters to enforce their sexual prejudices through law. Tolerance is a basic value under laissez-faire capitalism, so this example of direct disregard for tolerance should have disturbed Scalia. Thus, not only does he misread the amendment, but he also goes so far as to misstate the attitude of the voters by calling them "tolerant" while they try to enforce their own sexual prejudices. The dissonance contained in Scalia's opinion rings loudly despite his attempt to use rhetorical flourishes to distract the reader from the underlying inconsistency in his opinion.

There is no better example of the inconsistency of American-style laissez-faire capitalism than Scalia's opinion in *Romer*. It exposes the true values that underlie his often-stated commitment to formal equality. Sexual moralism excuses adherence to the constitutional principles of equality under the law.

### Statutory Law

#### SEX DISCRIMINATION

When Ernest Dillon[39] and Mario Carreno[40] were subjected to repeated graffiti with statements such as "Dillon gives head" or had their genitals and buttocks caressed by coworkers, they were denied protection under Title VII of the Civil Rights Act of 1964 because their claims were considered to be based on sexual orientation rather than gender. (Title VII prohibits employment discrimination on the basis of sex.) They were not allowed to use Title VII to gain protection for themselves as gay men. Yet when Robin McCoy, a female, brought suit under Title VII because her female supervisor allegedly rubbed McCoy's breasts, rubbed between McCoy's legs, and forced her tongue into McCoy's mouth while also calling McCoy "stupid poor white trash" and "stupid poor white bitch," McCoy prevailed.[41] Instead of branding the case as one based on sexual orientation, the court found that it fit the standard rules for sexual harassment. U.S. courts have therefore allowed Title VII to be used *against* lesbian or gay male supervisor-employees but have not allowed Title VII to be used on their behalf.

This complicated web of caselaw makes sense when one appreciates the moralistic agenda underlying the courts' interpretation of Title VII. Title VII is interpreted to protect the chastity of heterosexual women and protect heterosexual men from sexual advances from other men. But it is not designed to extend any comparable protection to gay men and lesbians. No matter how horrendously they are sexualized at the workplace, they do not receive protection from such sexualization by the courts. It is only those persons who are perceived by the courts to be heterosexuals who receive protection from sexualization.

Application of pure laissez-faire principles would, of course, result in the repeal of Title VII. And Richard Epstein, as a pure proponent of such principles, does call for the repeal of all antidiscrimination laws.[42] But Epstein's approach is not the dominant approach under American law. Instead, the courts interpret existing antidiscrimination doctrine to advance a homophobic, moralistic agenda.

This awkward interpretation of Title VII is not inevitable

under capitalism. Canadian courts have not excluded gay and lesbian workers from the law of sex discrimination. Whereas U.S. courts have refused to find that gay and lesbian people are protected against same-sex harassment at the workplace, Canadian courts have found that such harassment is unlawful. In *Re Cami Automotive Inc. and Canadian Auto Workers, Local 88*,[43] the arbitrator assumed that sexual harassment discrimination would violate the collective-bargaining agreement. The only issue in dispute was a technical one—whether the griever had given sufficient notice of his inability to work because of the harassment. While finding that he had not given sufficient notice at the time, the arbitrator found that he should have been reinstated when a psychiatrist finally provided justification more than six months later. Unlike the United States, here the context for the arbitrator was that both the collective-bargaining agreement and the human rights ordinance forbid sexual orientation discrimination.

## EMPLOYMENT NONDISCRIMINATION ACT

Because the courts have refused to interpret the U.S. Constitution or Title VII as extending protection to gay men and lesbians, the only legal recourse for gay men and lesbians has been to persuade the legislature to pass new statutes to protect them. In the last several years, a key strategy of the gay rights movement has been to gain passage of the Employment Nondiscrimination Act (ENDA)—a federal statute designed to provide protection from employment discrimination for gay men and lesbians.

To gain passage of this statute under a Republican Congress, the proponents have had to draft the statute quite narrowly to make it minimally acceptable to American politicians. They have tried to structure the statute around laissez-faire principles by having it reflect principles of formal equality and intrude as little as possible into the economy of the workplace.

Knowing that any affirmative rights for gay and lesbian people would immediately receive a strong negative response, the drafters of ENDA carefully eliminated any vestiges of affirmative treatment in the statute. Thus the statute generally provides that employers not be permitted to "discriminate against an individual on the basis of sexual orientation." The two possible "special treatment" arguments that may have been made against the statute were specifically eliminated through the statutory language. First, Section 5 of the statute provides that it "does not apply to the provision of employee benefits to an individual for the benefit of such individual's partner." In other words, employers can continue to offer health insurance benefits to the partners of heterosexuals but not to the partners of gay people despite the passage of ENDA. Second, Section 7 of the statute provides that a "covered entity shall not adopt or implement a quota on the basis of sexual orientation" and that a "covered entity shall not give preferential treatment to an individual on the basis of sexual orientation." Even voluntary affirmative action becomes unlawful under ENDA, although it is not entirely unlawful under Title VII.

Not only does the statute not require (or even permit) any type of "special treatment," but it also exempts the armed services and religious institutions from coverage, thereby honoring the twin principles of moralism and militarism. The net effect of these exclusions and qualifications is that many of the gay rights issues that are currently being hotly litigated—gays in the military and health insurance benefits for same-sex couples—are not affected by the passage of ENDA. Nonetheless, during the 1996 presidential election campaign, Senator Robert

Dole, the Republican candidate, criticized ENDA as a "special treatment" statute. When asked during the second presidential debate whether he supported the "Employment Nondiscrimination Act" (ENDA) (which would ban discrimination on the basis of sexual orientation in the workplace), Senator Dole responded that he did not favor "special rights for any group,"[44] strongly implying that ENDA constituted "special treatment legislation." But of course, ENDA cannot be arguably characterized as special treatment legislation.

An interesting question is what the implications of the exclusions and exceptions found in the current version of ENDA are. Can any classwide effects be discerned from the compromises that were made in the hope of ENDA's eventual passage under American capitalism? The employee benefit exclusion is important to those members of the gay community who live in a household in which one person holds health insurance benefits and the other person does not. Since  middle-class full-time employees are more likely to have health insurance benefits, this problem is usually the most serious in households in which one partner holds a blue-collar job, works part time, or is unemployed. Women, on average, have less lucrative jobs than do men. Thus, a relationship consisting of two women is much more likely to face this problem than a household consisting of two men. The AIDS crisis has also, of course, disproportionately affected gay men. To the extent that the AIDS crisis has also impoverished households after one partner becomes unable to work but still must seek medical treatment, this exclusion will affect many poor households consisting of two men.

The AIDS crisis has caused many people in the gay community to begin to support a system of nationalized health insurance, because they now realize how important the health insurance issue is to basic survival. But when the gay community itself proposes national antidiscrimination legislation, it ironically finds that it cannot mention health insurance for fear that such a measure would derail the entire bill. In other words, capitalist opposition to national health insurance seeps into the debate about a nondiscrimination bill that covers the private sector. (In the same presidential debate, Senator Dole was careful to link the Democrats with support of national health insurance—something he thought flew in the face of American capitalism for most voters. He therefore was playing the capitalism card.)

The impact of affirmative action language might also be felt on a class-defined basis. First, we must ask, Where does affirmative action currently exist that it might end? Few mainstream employers have any kind of affirmative action program that includes gay people. In the gay community, one might argue that gay-owned businesses such as bars, clubs, and restaurants have affirmative action policies in that they are likely to want to hire "one of their own" to work at establishments that cater to the gay community. Furthermore, such businesses probably offer salaries at the low end of the wage spectrum, since service jobs are usually low paying. The effect of ENDA might be to generate reverse discrimination cases against gay-owned establishments. Even if these establishments did not have any formal or informal policy of favoring gay applicants, a heterosexual may be able to convince a conservative judge or jury that such a policy existed. (Given the way that Title VII has been used to harm gay men and lesbians, this result would not be surprising.) Thus, ENDA might foster an attack on gay institutions while having a disproportionate impact on gay men and lesbians who hold such service-industry jobs. (For example,

Michael Hardwick's job as a bartender in a gay bar would be in jeopardy.)

Nondiscrimination legislation on the basis of sexual orientation in Canada has not suffered from these kinds of class-based problems. Unlike the American model, in which a new statute was drafted to respond to sexual orientation discrimination, Canadian provinces tackled the problem of discrimination against gay men and lesbians by amending their existing nondiscrimination legislation to include sexual orientation. Since the existing nondiscrimination laws in Canada do protect affirmative action, the amendment of those laws to include sexual orientation does not prevent affirmative action on the basis of sexual orientation. The health care issue in Canada does not pose the same level of problem for gay and lesbian people in Canada as it does in the United States, because all people have health insurance through their provincial government, regardless of their employment or familial status. Family-related issues arise only with respect to supplemental benefits, for instance, dental or vision insurance, that may not be offered as part of the minimum provincial plan. These supplemental benefits are sometimes provided through employers and, as in the United States, not necessarily made available to the same-sex partners of employees.

At first glance, the American law of sexual orientation appears to be chaotic. But when one examines the law through the lens of moralism and militarism, it comes into focus. When faced with an issue affecting gay men and lesbians, conservatives like Justice Scalia abandon laissez-faire economic principles. And when the American military needs to be defended, the U.S. Congress and the courts abandon laissez-faire economic principles.

But these results are not inevitable under capitalism. Although other capitalist countries are managing to extend constitutional and statutory protection to gay men and lesbians, there is little sign of change in the United States, notwithstanding the decision in *Romer v. Evans* and the progress being made toward the passage of ENDA.

# 6

## UNPROTECTED WORKERS

In the late 1980s, Michael Anthony Bullard worked for Bigelow
Holding Company, a rental company in the state of Nevada.[1]
Bullard believed that the company had a rental policy of discriminating against African Americans. On one occasion, he
feared that the company was planning to physically assault two
black men who had entered the property in order to get them
out. When his coemployee, Carol Swenson, radioed his supervisor, Donna Dollman, about the presence of the black men on the
property, Bullard said to Swenson, "Blacks have rights, too."
After Swenson reported that remark to Dollman, Dollman
entered the office and said to Bullard: "What's your fucking
problem?" "I don't have a problem," replied Bullard. Dollman
said, "I think you do. I think you're a fucking nigger lover. Sit
your God damn ass down on that fucking stool, shut your

mouth, and do your fucking work." Less then a minute later, Dollman added, "On second thought, get your fucking ass out of here. I don't want you working for me anymore."

Bullard, a blue-collar, nonunion employee, sued his employer for unlawful discharge. Although a jury was sympathetic to his case and awarded damages for a discharge that was contrary to public policy, the Supreme Court of Nevada reversed the ruling in a 1995 decision, declaring that Bullard's discharge was not governed by federal nondiscrimination law and that he did not have any contractual protection from arbitrary discharge. Like most American workers, he was employed "at will" and could be discharged for any reason at all. According to the Nevada Supreme Court, Bullard could be discharged simply because the employer considered him to a "a bad person, a person who was sympathetic to African-Americans."

Few people in the United States receive federally mandated protection from arbitrary treatment at the workplace. Although Title VII of the Civil Rights Act of 1964 protects against discrimination on the basis of race, sex, national origin, and religion, these claims are rarely successful except for reverse discrimination claims brought by white men. By imposing an impossible threshold of proof on the plaintiffs, judges dispose of many discrimination claims brought by women and minorities by rendering summary judgments in favor of the defendants, thereby precluding these cases from even going to the jury.[2] Similarly, the Americans with Disabilities Act purports to protect against discrimination on the basis of disability, yet as we saw in chapter 3, narrow legal decisions have rendered most of these claims to be unsuccessful even when strong evidence of discrimination exists. Mandatory arbitration clauses have also prevented many victims of discrimination from receiving their "day in court."[3] Instead, they have been subjected to employer-biased arbitrators.[4] And those employees whose discharge claims that lie outside American antidiscrimination law have virtually no legal recourse.

The United States is the only Western industrialized nation that still operates under the premises of the "employment at will" doctrine, by which employers need not demonstrate "cause" to fire an employee. (The United States also is the only Western nation not to ratify Convention 158 of the International Labor Organization, which forbids employers from terminating employees without just cause.)[5] In the hands of conservative judges, this doctrine gives nearly unlimited leeway to employers to fire employees. In one case, Judge Posner concluded that a chief executive officer was a "master of vengefulness" as well as a "bad man" but nonetheless was justified in firing a sixty-two-year-old employee who refused to pledge loyalty to him because the chief executive was stealing from the firm.[6] Laissez-faire economics seems to require no respect for basic human or civil rights at the workplace.

The employment-at-will doctrine is only one of several policies that leaves many employees without meaningful protection at the workplace. Unpaid and underpaid domestic workers, part-time employees, and employees who work for small employers are often excluded from the protection of federal law.

As economists Barry Bluestone and Bennett Harrison asked, "How do we build a stable, humane, equitable community and still have economic growth? And how do we go about the business of constructing a productive economy which produces livelihoods without destroying lives?"[7] Unfortunately, the response of American capitalism to these questions has been disappointing; community has been sacrificed for capital.

## Underpaid Domestic Workers

In March 1986, a native of Trinidad, was hired as the babysitter for Judge Kimba Wood's infant son. Because the babysitter was not a legal resident of the United States, domestic work was one of the only occupations for which she could legally qualify—it was not until later that year that Congress passed a law making it illegal to employ illegal aliens as domestic help.[8] By then, her employer had completed the necessary paperwork to employ her legally. The sitter's resident status, however, depended on her retaining her job as a babysitter. Unlike most babysitters, her employer even paid her Social Security taxes.

Zoe Baird's babysitter wasn't treated quite as well. She, too, was an illegal alien who was paid $250 per week to care for her infant. Unlike Kimba Wood, her employer failed to pay Social Security taxes and workers' compensation taxes (until her non-payment became politically embarrassing). Like Wood, however, Baird and her husband sponsored the woman for status as a lawful resident, giving her the opportunity to stay in this poorly paid job.

The Baird and Wood incidents put the spotlight on the plight of illegal aliens who work as domestic help in rich people's households. The political response, however, was to relieve the burden on rich people by extending the Social Security exemption for domestic work rather than to improve the situation of illegal aliens who have few employment opportunities other than potentially exploitive domestic work. (Could these illegal aliens have complained about unlawful or even criminal treatment?—Not if they wanted to stay in the United States.) No attempt was made to broaden the enforcement of the Social Security or Immigration laws to protect the interests of domestic workers. Even the National Organization for Women (NOW) did not see this episode as an opportunity to comment on the deplorable conditions for domestic workers. Instead Patricia Ireland, NOW's president, complained about this incident as "just too clear an example of a double standard being used to keep women out of power."[9] The solution is apparently to allow women to exploit domestic labor as much as men have historically exploited it. That is, laissez-faire economics is such a powerful discipline in the United States that even the National Organization for Women has trouble seeing past its distorted consequences.

American households have little to fear from employing illegal aliens (unless one of the parents decides to seek a highly publicized political appointment) because the Immigration and Naturalization Service (INS) does not target households for investigation. Moreover, the fines rarely exceed $1,000. Thus, American households can afford to ignore immigration law (and all other laws) when hiring household help, whereas illegal aliens have few other employment options. The Immigration Reform and Control Act of 1986 (making unlawful the hiring of illegal aliens as domestic workers) coupled with the Immigration Act of 1990 (greatly increasing the waiting period for household workers to obtain permanent status) and the INS's policy of not enforcing its laws against households leaves a patchwork of subsidization for upper-class American households and exploitation for poor women from Third World countries.

The Baird and Wood incidents are only some of the most recent examples of overlooked exploitation of domestic workers.

American law and politics has historically disregarded the conditions of domestic work. The Fair Labor Standards Act (FLSA) was first passed in 1938, but over a storm of laissez-faire opposition. Like the modern-day Family and Medical Leave Act, the original FLSA was more promise than action. It set a twenty-five-cents-per-hour federal minimum wage for some employees working in interstate commerce, which affected the wages of only 300,000 employees in the United States. Large classes of employees were exempted from the statute: workers in intrastate industries (such as domestic workers); workers in executive, administrative, professional or local retail; workers in retail or service industries operating in intrastate commerce; seamen, air carrier workers; workers in the fishing and seafood-processing industry; anyone in agriculture; people in dairy processing; workers for small newspapers; local bus or trolley workers; and learners, apprentices, and handicapped workers. Predominantly female occupations such as those of hotel workers, retail clerks, janitors, nurses, and domestic workers were excluded from coverage. The agricultural exclusion disproportionately affected southern African Americans. "Because of these exemptions, the employees protected by the FLSA were predominantly white, male, industrial-class workers. Indeed, the 1938 FLSA was politically crafted to exclude many workers from its minimum-wage coverage, particularly women and southern African-American workers."[10]

Although today, some of these initial gaps in coverage have been filled, the FLSA still exempts employees of seasonal amusement businesses, people in outside sales, domestic workers, some agricultural and seafood workers, some employees of small newspapers, and some retail and service workers. When the Clinton administration supported raising the minimum wage, no consideration was given to filling in those gaps. Thus, minimum wage laws leave domestic workers underpaid and underprotected by the law.

Minimum wage laws are not the only laws that fail to apply to domestic workers. Many states exclude domestic workers along with other contingent workers from unemployment insurance programs.[11] Similarly, the Occupational Safety and Health Act (OSHA) does not cover domestic workers if they are not considered "employees" or if their immediate worksite is not an "employer' under the law. The restrictive tenure and vesting requirements make the Employee Retirement Income Security Act unavailable to domestic workers. All the federal legislation that contains requirements for minimum numbers of employees—such as Title VII of the Civil Rights Act of 1964 (fifteen employees), the Americans with Disabilities Act (fifteen employees), and the Family and Medical Leave Act (fifty employees)—also excludes domestic workers. Thus, from 1938 onward, we see a continuing trend to exclude domestic workers from any statutory protection.

The immigration law supports the abuse of domestic workers, as it makes it almost impossible for unskilled workers (which is how domestic workers are classified) to immigrate legally to the United States to secure employment.[12] Even if they have a household sponsor, it typically takes ten years for their application to be approved. A household employer who needs a domestic worker can rarely afford to wait that long. Consequently, as "Nannygate" revealed, many households hire aliens illegally to work in their households because, in practice, the employers of domestic workers are rarely targeted for "employer sanctions," or I-9, violations. Therefore, even though household employers have little to fear in regard to the law's enforcement, illegal aliens have much to fear. If an employer violates the minimum wage or maximum hour laws or, more significantly, subjects them to sexual abuse, they face deportation if they complain about the violation of their rights. Such workers do not, of course, have any "rights" given their illegal status.

Who benefits from these rules? The public controversy about "Nannygate" clarifies who the intended beneficiaries are. These exclusions make it easier for the upper class to afford the services of domestic workers. When Zoe Baird had legal problems because she underpaid her taxes for her domestic worker, the response was to broaden the exemption for paying taxes for domestic workers. The political response to the Baird/Wood episode should have been a commitment to strenghtening the protection for domestic workers rather than expanding the loopholes for the upper class.

### Unpaid Domestic Workers

In 1984, at the age of sixty-two, Gladyce Cornelius began regularly caring for her granddaughter while her daughter was employed at the Alabama Institute for the Deaf and Blind.[13] In 1986, her daughter began paying her mother for these services at the modest rate of $45 per week. She also made contributions to Social Security on behalf of her mother. When she reached the age of sixty-five, Cornelius tried to collect these Social Security retirement benefits. Her claim was denied, however, because her earnings for babysitting services were not covered, since they were performed in the home of her daughter. The Social Security Act's regulations exempt such services from statutory coverage, even though the Eleventh Circuit concluded that the Social Security Act rule was based on the presumption "that there is no need for domestic service when both spouses are present and able to work." Congress apparently assumed that under these circumstances, the woman works in the home and the man in the marketplace. Nonetheless, the court found that the statute did not violate the equal protection clause. Under the act, a parent may work for his child in the course of the child's trade or business but may not perform domestic services for the child either inside or outside the home.[14] Domestic services have not qualified as genuine "work" under American law.

Under American law, housework has never been considered to have economic value.[15] Work in the home thus provides no entitlement to Social Security, is not included in the gross domestic product, and is unvalued or grossly undervalued at the time of divorce. Despite the public rhetoric to the contrary, welfare moms do "work," supervising and nurturing children. They are poor partly because as a society, we do not compensate such work, but this does not make the work less genuine.

In the name of laissez-faire economics, American politicians increasingly proclaim that poor mothers* should receive no subsidy from the state. Such a subsidy, we are told, creates a "cycle of dependency" that undermines American families and work ethic. Welfare mothers are supposed to be lazy women who stay home all day using drugs and abusing their children. But, in fact,

> while welfare pays badly, low-wage jobs pay even worse. Most welfare mothers are quite willing to work if they end up with significantly more disposable income as a result. But they are not willing to work if working will leave them as poor as they were when they stayed home.[16]

---

*Throughout this discussion, I refer to "mother," since these policies disproportionately affect women who are raising children. Of course, I realize that some men are single parents and so are also affected by these policies.

Even more important, why should we give these women an incentive to work in the public marketplace while raising young children? The same data that support paid leave for women who work in the marketplace also support subsidies for women who work in the home—that is, children benefit from parental care in the first year of their lives. Poor women, like upper-class women, should be able to choose to stay home to care for their own children without feeling economically coerced to enter the marketplace. In fact, society may disproportionately benefit from having poor women stay home to care for their children because such care might help their children counter the influence of "drugs, crime, gangs, and other lethal lures" to which their children are routinely exposed. "If motherhood in general entails work, poor motherhood entails even more work, and poor motherhood, while receiving AFDC, is one of the most burdensome types of motherhood imaginable."[17]

The subsidies sought by single mothers with children are no different from the subsidies sought from other, more acceptable family constellations in our society. To qualify for federal assistance, a poor woman must be both the head of a household and responsible for dependent children. Her work is domestic work—taking care of her children.

If this woman were married to a wage-earning spouse, we would be happy as a society to subsidize her child care. Under our tax code, married families with only one wage earner receive a marriage benefit and also can deduct their children as "dependents." If they buy a house, they also can take advantage of generous tax mortgage policies. And if they both enter the workforce and need to pay for child care, they can also take a tax deduction for that expense, thereby receiving state assistance in paying for their child care. Thus, either the family is subsidized for having the woman stay at home, or the family is subsidized for their child care while she works outside the home.

U.S. law tries simultaneously to cut back benefits to single mothers on welfare while increasing child-based tax deductions for middle-class Americans. Assistance to poor mothers is stigmatized, and assistance to middle-class families is applauded. The American approach to subsidizing parenthood is relatively unusual. Most countries in the West provide a child allowance or basic income guarantee to all families with children, not just to the poor. Caretaking benefits are considered as earned income, regardless of the care provider's social or economic class. In the United States, we hold children hostage while we use our social welfare policies to impose on poor mothers the values of marriage and male dependency. "Like the war on drugs, the war on poverty, now recast as the war on welfare, has the underlying passion of a moral crusade."[18] It is time that we recognize the economic value of raising children, regardless of the parent's marital status or economic class.

### The Contingent Workforce

Jere Ellis, an employee of Charles Raines, fell 985 feet to his death while painting a television tower owned by Chase Communications.[19] At the time of his fall, his only protective equipment was a short belt safety harness, which Ellis had unhooked in order to change positions on the tower. His estate filed a suit against the owner of the premises on which he fell to his death, claiming that Chase had not ensured that the work met the standards set by the federal Occupational Safety and Health Act (OSHA). Because Chase had hired an independent contractor to perform the work on the tower, it was not subject to the requirements of OSHA. Jere Ellis, like many persons who work in inherently dangerous occupations, received little legal protection under federal or state law. Independent contractors, as well as all persons who perform domestic tasks at private residences, are excluded from protection under OSHA.[20] As part of the "contingent work force," they lie outside the law.

The contingent labor force—part-time workers, contract workers, temporary workers, and independent contractors—comprises almost a third of American workers.[21] The largest segment of the contingent workforce is part-time workers, many of whom in fact work full-time hours but do so by holding two or more part-time jobs. Part-time employees disproportionately earn the minimum wage (25 percent of them earn the minimum wage, compared with 5 percent of full-time workers). Employers who use contract workers avoid responsibility for tax withholdings of any kind and need not follow the law with regard to minimum wages and payment for overtime.

The use of contract workers has increased dramatically in the past two decades as employers have tried to downsize and save expenses.[22] Contract workers are most commonly found in low-paying industries such as construction, janitorial services, and garment manufacturing. Employers who use independent contractors avoid complying with safety regulations, paying payroll taxes and federally mandated benefits, and complying with standards such as unemployment benefits, workers' compensation, pension regulation, antidiscrimination laws, federal disability insurance, and minimum wage and maximum hour laws. Although some independent contractors are well-paid professionals, many are low-wage workers whose employers deliberately mislabel them as independent contractors to avoid compliance with various federal laws. One of the largest categories of poorly paid independent contractors is day laborers, disproportionately composed of immigrant men who work in construction, landscaping, agriculture, or other hazardous trades.[23]

According to former Labor Secretary Robert Reich, "The contingent workforce is outside the system of worker-management relationships and expectations we've created over the years."[24] The laws regulating working conditions, wages, hours, benefits and labor representation "implicitly reflect an increasingly outdated model of employment: full-time, long-term—even lifetime—employment with a single employer. Social welfare policy also remains largely predicated on this model."[25] Whereas 17.8 percent of all full-time workers belonged to a union in 1993, only 7.2 percent of part-timers were union members. The Employee Retirement and Income Security Act of 1981 (ERISA) requires only those employers who have a pension plan to extend it to all employees working more than one thousand hours per year (about twenty hours per week), and loopholes even allow employers to exclude part-time workers who average more than one thousand hours per year. The Family and Medical Leave Act excludes part-time workers from coverage even if their employer is covered. Employees are not eligible to receive Social Security retirement benefits or disability insurance even if their employer has contributed to Social Security on their behalf, unless they have been in "covered" employment earning above a statutory minimum amount for six of the previous thirteen quarters before seeking benefits. State-enforced programs also often fail to protect the contingent workforce. Temporary workers, domestic workers, and independent contractors are usually excluded from unemployment insurance programs, and minimum-work requirements often serve to exclude part-time employees.

The part-time labor force, though denied the protections of the social safety net, is often not voluntarily working part time. In 1993, 6 million Americans were involuntarily working part time. One-third of women working part time would work more hours if they could get child care. In general, part-time work in the United States is relatively poorly compensated, with few, if any, benefits. On average, full-time workers in the United States earn 39 percent more in hourly wages than do part-time workers. Of families headed by women (and therefore subject to the new restrictions on welfare), "half of these women who worked part-time in 1983 said they would rather have worked full-time but were constrained by the high costs and unavailability of quality child care."[26] If women who head households and are working only part time find it impractical to work full time, how can we expect women who head households and are unemployed to find manageable full-time employment? At most, we can probably expect these women to enter the ranks of the poorly compensated, part-time labor force.

The differential between part-time and full-time workers is much smaller in other industrialized countries. In the 1980s, 18 percent of Canada's part-time workers belonged to a union, and its full-time workers earned only 21 percent more on average than did part-time workers. Many countries, including France, Germany, and Spain, have laws forbidding discrimination in salary or benefits between part-time and full-time workers. Whereas U.S. law explicitly exempts part-time employees from most federal legislation, these countries mandate nondiscrimination between part-time and full-time workers. Not surprisingly, when Congresswoman Patricia Schroeder introduced the Part-Time and Temporary Workers Protection Act of 1993, publications like the *Wall Street Journal* complained loudly. Previous attempts to require full-time/part-time benefit parity have failed. Conservative economists typically praise the large part-time workforce in the United States as demonstrating the "flexiblility" of the U.S. economy, without assessing the voluntariness of that status or the level of compensation offered to those workers.[27]

## Employment at Will

### INDIVIDUAL TERMINATIONS

In 1989, Ruby Wells and two other licensed practical nurses who worked for a nursing home requested a meeting with the nursing home administrator to discuss problems at the workplace.[28] When the administrator refused to meet with them at that time, they drove to Toledo, Ohio, to meet with the director of human resources and vice president of operations. Two of the three nurses who made the trip to Toledo were terminated or disciplined, and so they filed a charge with the National Labor Relations Board claiming that they had been disciplined for engaging in concerted protected conduct for the purpose of collective bargaining. In a five-to-four decision, the U.S. Supreme Court ruled that they were not covered by the National Labor Relations Act because their duties included the supervision of nursing aides.[29] Receiving no protection from federal law, these nurses were "at will" employees who could be disciplined or terminated for any reason whatsoever, even though the administrative law judge had concluded that the licensed practical nurses were "just hired hands." Their predicament was typical of that of most American workers—they received virtually no workplace protection from discipline or discharge.

U.S. law is dominated by the principle of "employment at will," by which employers can fire workers without establishing cause, unless the employee is fortunate enough to have a contract specifying that justification is required for terminating a contract. The standard formulation for employment at will is that an employer may dismiss an employee "for good cause, for no cause, or even for cause morally wrong."[30] It is estimated that between 150,000 and 200,000 persons are dismissed in the United States each year without just cause, often with a resulting loss in health insurance.[31]

The at-will doctrine is a peculiarly American invention and is highly reflective of a laissez-faire attitude toward low-level workers. The doctrine was devised in 1877 by a New York attorney, H. G. Wood, in a scholarly treatise. He "announced as a general law in the U.S. the right of either employer or employee to terminate a contract of unspecified duration at any time, with or without cause, or even for bad cause."[32] The rationale behind the rule reflects the false presumptions underlying laissez-faire economics—that it is supposed to benefit worker and employer equally because they both are supposed to benefit equally from the flexibility to quit or be fired. But in reality, the rule disproportionately benefits the employer, who is much more likely to want to fire a worker than a worker is likely to want to quit.

Because of the harshness of the at-will rule for employees, the courts have created some—albeit very limited—exceptions to the principle. For example, an employee may expressly contract for a good cause requirement for discharge (outside the union context). Nonetheless, many courts have concluded that such a promise is not enforceable when it is found only in the employer-written personnel manual. The promise is considered to be "gratuitous" rather than binding in the absence of specific evidence that the employee relied on the promise when accepting the offer of employment.

One way to abolish the at-will doctrine would be through state contract law governing the employment relationship. Resistance to such a move in the United States, however, has been strong. Although the Uniform Law Commissioners' Model Termination Act, approved and recommended for adoption for all fifty state legislatures in 1991, abandoned the at-will doctrine, only one state (Montana) has enacted this proposed legislation. There is therefore little reason to believe that the at-will doctrine will be eliminated in the United States anytime soon.

The situation is markedly different in the European Union (EU). Of the fifteen countries included in the EU, all but Belgium and Greece require good cause for termination. In addition, each of these countries (especially including Belgium and Greece) require minimum pretermination notice periods. Most European countries have works councils. For example, Austria's works councils "must be consulted prior to any management action on certain measures specified by statute and in some instances the council must give its consent before a management decision may be implemented. One such requirement to obtain the work council's consent is termination, either with or without notice."[33] Thus, not only must management meet certain specified criteria before termination, but also the decision itself must be reviewed before it can become final.

The contrast between the United States and Europe reflects starkly different conceptions of employer freedom. In the United States, employers rarely have to justify their termination decisions. In Europe, however, the employer has the burden of proving to a works council that it has good cause for dismissal.

Although the American rule supposedly derived from the British common law, Great Britain has long since repudiated the doctrine. Since 1978, British employees have been statutorily protected from unfair dismissal by the Employment Protection (Consolidation) Act, under which the employer must demonstrate that he reasonably believed that the employee engaged in misconduct.

Similarly, in Germany, dismissals are legally void when they are "socially unjustified."[34] The employer has the burden to show justification, and disputes concerning justification are handled by the labor courts. The employer must also consult with the works council before dismissing an employee.

Sweden used the doctrine of employment at will until 1974 when it passed the Employment Security Act. Dismissals must now be based on "objective cause."[35] This standard is even stricter than the "good cause" standard used in the United States for employees governed by collective-bargaining agreements. As in Germany and Great Britain, the employer must inform the union before dismissing the employee and must give notice to the employee before dismissal. Additional notice must be given to the county employment board to enable the board to assist in finding future employment for the terminated worker. Terminated employees also receive a wide range of social services that are funded by the government rather than the employer.

Because of the harshness of the "at-will" doctrine that underlies American labor law, it is important for employees to contract for a "good cause" standard for discharge. One way to acquire such protection is through a union contract, which typically contains a good cause rule, as well as a grievance process to contest a discharge. Nonetheless, less than 20 percent of the American workforce is unionized. Some workers, like domestic workers, are nonunionized because they are not protected by the National Labor Relations Act. Other workers are technically eligible for collective-bargaining protection but do not belong to a union.

### COLLECTIVE DISMISSALS: PLANT CLOSINGS

First National Maintenance Corporation (FNMC) had an employment relationship with maintenance personnel who cleaned the Greenpark Care Center.[36] Under the terms of their contract, Greenpark was prohibited from directly hiring the workers during the term of their contract or for ninety days thereafter. Shortly before FNMC terminated its contract with the Greenpark Care Center, and thereby ended its employment relationship with those employees, the Greenpark employees joined a union. The employees were given three days' notice that their employment contract would be terminated, and they therefore tried to bargain with the employer to renegotiate their contract and retain their jobs. Although the company maintained that terminating the employment relationship was "purely a matter of money," it refused to negotiate with the union representative for the employees. The employees were fired and Greenpark was unable to hire the former FNM employees directly because of the contract's ninety-day limitation.

The union filed a grievance alleging that the employer had failed to engage in bargaining as required under the National Labor Relations Act. The administrative law judge held in favor of the union. The National Labor Relations Board adopted the findings of the administrative law judge. The employer appealed to the U.S. Court of Appeals for the Second Circuit, which enforced the board's order in a two-to-one decision. The U.S. Supreme Court reversed. Applying a balancing test, it concluded that "the harm likely to be done to an employer's need to operate freely in deciding whether to shut down part of its business purely for economic reasons outweighs the incremental benefit that might be gained through the union's participation in making the decision."

The Court never seriously contemplated the value to the employees of, at least, negotiating to have the ninety-day rule eliminated, so that Greenpark could hire them directly. Such an agreement would have produced a potentially significant benefit to the employees while gaining FNM a modest public relations benefit for no cost. Or more significantly, as pointed out by the dissenting justices, the union might have been "able to offer concessions, information, and alternatives that might obviate or forestall the closing."[37] The majority nonetheless ignored contemporaneous experiences at other workplaces at which such negotiations had been productive, choosing instead to speculate that the benefit of such negotiations was minimal. As judges with lifetime tenure, the majority seemed unable to consider the costs and benefits for the employees in this case. Once again, an opinion tainted with the cost-benefit scheme of law and economics holds for the employer-entrepreneur.

The law on plant closings has improved only modestly in the United States since the Greenpark case was decided in 1981. Congress passed the Worker Adjustment and Retraining Notification Act in 1988,[38] which requires a sixty-day notice to employees before a plant may close or engage in a mass layoff, but in most situations, the exceptions to this rule undercut its effectiveness.

To be covered by the statute, an employer must lay off at least one-third of the employees, constituting at least either fifty employees at one site or at least five hundred employees. Thus, even if an employer has hundreds of employees at dozens of different sites but no closed site has more than fifty employees, he is not covered by the statute, which results in the exclusion of major industries such as trucking and delivery services.[39]

Very large employers are also often able to escape coverage under the five-hundred-employee layoff rule. For example, McDonnell Douglas Corporation laid off 609 employees between October 16, 1992, and January 14, 1993, but through clever counting rules was able to escape the five-hundred-employee rule (some employees were part time; some worked about eleven miles from the main plant; some were rehired within six months).[40] Employers may reduce the notification period if they are actively seeking capital or business in order to avoid a shutdown or if the business circumstances requiring the layoff were not reasonably foreseeable. The unforeseeable business circumstances exception has been construed generously, allowing McDonnell Douglas to argue that it could not foresee the cancellation of a fighter/bomber contract, although its own long-standing performance problems were clearly a major factor in the cancellation of the contract. Moreover, testimony before Congress had forewarned it of the slowdown in government military contracts long before this happened. Despite more than six months of negotiations with the government, which resulted in the cancellation of the contract, the court concluded that McDonnell Douglas met the standard of a "sudden, dramatic, and unexpected action or condition" leading to an economic downturn.[41]

It is unlikely that the Greenpark employees would have

received any protection had this statute existed at the time of their layoff in the early 1980s, because their situation could not be described as a "mass layoff." Moreover, the relief that they sought—the ability to negotiate directly with another contractor—is not contemplated in this federal statute. They also may not have had the required fifty statutory employees.

Whereas European countries try to prevent plant closings and assist workers who lose jobs because of plant closings, American law perversely encourages plant closings. The U.S. Steel Corporation, for example, could close down fourteen mills in eight states, laying off thirteen thousand workers, for a $850 million tax break, which it later put toward the down payment on the purchase of Marathon Oil.[42]

The era of Reaganomics saw a bidding war among the states to lower the tax rates on corporations while also cutting back protections for employees. Companies are not subtle about the business climate they seek—at the expense of workers. For example, the Conference of State Manufacturers Association ranked Mississippi as having the best "business climate" because it had low taxes, low union membership, low workers' compensation insurance rates, low unemployment benefits per worker, low energy costs, and few days lost work because of stoppages.[43] Where favorable benefits do not already exist, companies are able to extract them from cities or states. General Motors, for example, "convinced" the city of Detroit to clear four hundred acres of land, dislocating 3,200 people from one of Detroit's most socially integrated communities and closing 160 community businesses while giving GM a twelve-year tax abatement worth $240 million in forgone revenues to build a new plant. In the unbalanced world in which American corporations do business, communities have little choice but to make such concessions. If they do not, companies can quickly relocate to communities that will provide these and other concessions.

American workers receive almost no protection from plant closings. Less than 10 percent of employees have contracts that provide for advance notification before a plant is closed. And of those workers with prenotification rules, more than three-fourths are guaranteed only a one-week notice or less. Rarely are employees entitled to any severance pay. Of the minority of employees covered by a contract, only half receive any severance pay.

By contrast, most European countries require employers to negotiate layoffs with the employees' union or joint labor-management council. If layoffs are unavoidable, corporations are required to give advance notice to the workers, the unions, and the national employment service before closing a plant or dismissing workers for economic reasons. In Germany, the Co-determination Act of 1976 requires a company contemplating a shutdown to open its books to the local works council so that it can evaluate its corporate data. If a plant must close, a one-year advance notice must be provided. Other rules also mitigate the effect of collective dismissals. Employers are required to take into account "social aspects" when dismissing employees, thereby requiring those who would suffer most from dismissal to be the last to be let go.[44] Employers must also give employees the opportunity to transfer jobs even if the new job would require some schooling or training. Finally, when an employer with twenty or more employees plans a substantial change in the workforce, the employer and works council are required to work out a "social plan" to accommodate the interests of workers as much as possible, including the awarding of severance pay.

In Great Britain, employers must give advance notice of dismissal, depending on the length of prior employment. The employer must also give those being dismissed two days off with pay to look for other work. As in Germany, the employer is required to consult with the employees' representative before making decisions on collective dismissals. In the event of dismissals, severance pay is required. Whereas federal and local government provide incentives for corporation relocation in the United States, European policy seeks to avoid such relocation.

Repeated attempts to pass meaningful national plant-closing laws in the United States have been unsuccessful. Not surprisingly, the business community has opposed such legislation, saying that it would be impractical because shutdown decisions are often made abruptly. Case studies reveal, however, that most shutdown decisions are planned far in advance, and both American and European companies that do business in Europe find it possible to abide by those countries' shutdown rules.[45]

The only hope for increased employee protection against plant closings in the United States appears to be on the state level. Some states have passed plant-closing legislation that typically provides for assistance to unemployed workers after a plant has closed rather than trying to avert the plant closing itself. Even such minimal legislation often excludes many businesses; the Tennessee statute, for example, oddly covers only businesses with more than fifty but fewer than ninety-nine employees.[46] States that enact legislation that tries to limit plant closings would be on the list of communities that are inhospitable to business. And one can only hope that the courts would not water down such legislation through narrow interpretations so as to undermine the protections intended by such laws.

The U.S. economy is a subsidized economy. The real question is which sectors receive subsidy. In the employment arena, we subsidize those workers and employers who least need subsidies and cut back on subsidies to the poor. Rather than exclude domestic and agricultural workers from most employment protections, we need to put such workers in the forefront of state protection because they are least likely to be able to contract for protection from their employer. Rather than stigmatize parenting for the poor, we need to recognize the work inherent in all parenting. Such proposals are not outlandish; they are fundamental in other Western industrialized countries.

# 7

## MEDINA'S STORY

Consider these two fictional accounts, one from our past and one that imagines our future:

*Isabelle's daughter, Medina, attended the local college whose in-state tuition she could afford to pay. Eventually she enrolled in law school and graduated with honors. She decided to seek a clerkship so that she could someday enter the legal academy. Hearing that there was an opening in the local state court judge's chambers, she applied for a job. Aware that political connections often were important to securing a state clerk courtship (since state court judges are elected), she nonetheless hoped she would have a decent shot at selection, owing to her strong academic record and racial diversity. She had done some research on this particular judge, a Judge Johnson, and thus knew he was eager to win the Latino vote in the next election. He might, she hoped, therefore be interested in hiring a Latina clerk.*

*A few weeks after sending in her application, Medina received a telephone call from Johnson's secretary inviting her to come in for an interview. Medina was thrilled and immediately began to think about planning a successful interview. Her friends recommended that she ditch the corn rows for some hair straightener and buy a conventional blue suit. They also suggested she be careful in handling the diversity issue because Johnson would not want to hire a clerk whom he viewed as a rabble-rouser or one who was overtly trying to capitalize on her ethnic status. And of course, they told her to keep quiet about her lesbianism; coming out of the closest was the surest way to kill a job interview.*

*Isabelle was torn. She took pride in her "natural" looks and never was one to hide her sexual orientation. It did not seem fair that Johnson could value her for her diversity yet demand that she look "white." She also knew that even if she were hired, Johnson could fire her at any time without explanation. What if he learned of her lesbianism after she got the job and then fired her? Her partner, Elisa, was pregnant with twins, and it would probably be hard to hide these additions to her family, especially since she and Elisa had agreed that Medina would be the second parent on the birth certificate. She wanted to feel free to put pictures of her family on her desk at work just as the other law clerks did. As much as she needed the job, she also did not want a blotch on her record from being fired. She could send him her résumé that revealed her gay and lesbian legal work— that would get her "out of the closet" before the interview. But that strategy might also backfire—give him an excuse to turn* her down for the job before the interview. Usually, she had found, it was better to have people find out about her sexual orientation after they got to know her so that they could overcome their stereotypes. Maybe if she could find a discreet way to mention her lesbianism after making a good impression, it would work out. She did not want Judge Johnson to get angry at her later for trying to hide her lesbianism. This was a difficult dilemma but one she needed to resolve if she was to be a stable source of support for her ill mother and growing family and if she was to project herself as a confident and valuable prospect.

On the day of the interview, Medina sat down nervously in a chair in the Judge's chambers wearing her blue suit and with her hair pulled back away from her face. (With that hairstyle, she could avoid straightening chemicals.) The judge entered, giving her a smile that put her somewhat at ease.

"Thank you for coming in today. As you probably know, I interview only a few people for my clerkship, but I was very impressed with your record and references."

"Thank you," replied Medina, "I was thrilled to get the interview because I have been very impressed with your record as a judge. Not to sound like an apple polisher, but I remember thinking at the time that your decision last year in Sawyers v. Daniels was a real pathbreaker. I am sure that other state supreme courts will consider developing such a theory in their contract cases."

"Well, thank you. Yes, I must confess that I'm rather proud of that decision. The idea that an employer could not be bound by a statement in an employee handbook had bothered me for years. Sawyers v. Daniels gave me the ideal factual pattern to rule that employers must abide by the plant notification clauses in their handbooks. Those workers needed an opportunity to look elsewhere for employment or, if possible, try to raise the capital to run the plant themselves. But I put in the 'exceptional circumstances' clause so as not to tie the hands of employers in the event of unforeseeable circumstances. Clearly, in this case, the shutdown was long anticipated although unknown to the employees."

Well, mused the judge, she seems well informed about my decisions, even if it's only because she's done her homework. But I wonder if she can be objective about hard cases. Can she also help me draft opinions that are favorable to the employer? Her background suggests a strong employee bias. Maybe I should find out more about her background.

Pausing, the judge looked at Medina closely and said softly, "So, I see that you supported yourself through college and law school."

"Yes," replies Medina, "and I also had to support my mother who was no longer able to take care of herself. Given the years that my mother devoted to cleaning other people's houses so that I could buy books for high school and college, I figured that was the least that I could do."

"It must have been hard to live on so little."

"A lot of people seem to expect that my mother would have received state assistance, since she was disabled and over sixty-five. But she wasn't a U.S. citizen, so most benefits were not available to her."

"Uh, I hate to be nosy and perhaps it's not proper of me to ask, but I'm just wondering. Did she consider becoming a citizen in order to get some benefits?"

"My mother has always been a fiercely proud woman. When she was younger, she would not seek citizenship just to become eligible for benefits. She also assumed, somewhat pig-headedly, that she could work until the day she died. And then when she developed an extreme case of Alzheimer's, she no longer could meet the citizenship requirements."

"Did you try to get the government to waive some of the requirements in light of her disability?

"No, sir, there was no point. The United States never waives the requirement that you swear an oath of allegiance. And my mother's memory is so poor that she can't repeat the oath."

"I'm sorry to hear that. It's too bad Congress isn't more sensitive to those kinds of problems."

"That's not likely to change soon. My mother can't vote. My congressman isn't particularly concerned about her plight," said Medina, leaving out that she suspected this oversight was at least partially due to her accent.

"What about Social Security? Did her employer contribute to Social Security on her behalf?

"The law does require payment, of course, but it is almost never enforced. Enforcement against people like Zoe Baird is the exception, not the rule. It doesn't reflect the general enforcement pattern."

"Well, you certainly seem well informed about American law concerning the poor and immigrants. Do you have other specialized legal interests?"

"I find all of the law fascinating. I've had to learn poverty law and elderly law to assist my mother, but I honestly find nearly all aspects of the law stimulating. Maybe that's why I graduated with honors." Isabelle had to be careful not to show irritation in her voice. How many times had interviewers overlooked her strong record because of her special interest in the rights of the poor and the elderly?

"Um, yes, you're clearly a very fine student. Do you have other credentials that you think I might find of interest? Any references?"

"I belong to the Haitian Law Student Association and do volunteer work with them. I could give you a list of my clients to speak to. I also have written an amicus brief in an immigration case pending before the U.S. Supreme Court. I have a copy here with me."

"Thank you. I"ll be glad to look at that material. I'm happy to see your pro bono record, but I should caution you that you cannot do pro bono work while you clerk for me, because of the potential conflicts of interest. I also have to be careful not to bring any disrepute to this office, so I am very private about my political beliefs."

"Oh, I understand. I work with the Haitian group primarily for social reasons. It's a nice way to meet other Haitians."

"Of course, I encourage my clerks to be active in their church and social activities. But I also have to be very clear about the work rules. This is only a one-year position with no vacation time. I once had a clerk who, unknown to me at the interview, was three months pregnant when she started the job. Six months later, when it was time to give birth, she expected me to give her paid maternity leave for twelve weeks. There was just no way I could do that. I have a small office to run and very limited resources. If I had given her paid leave, then I would be short one clerk for twelve weeks. I offered to give her unpaid leave but rehire her the following year, because she was an excellent clerk. But she refused to see the situation from my position and was quite upset. So, now I'm very careful to tell people the rules up front. I'm a grandfather and love children, but I can't afford to extend leave of any kind to a clerk in my court. This may sound a bit harsh, but it's what the position and what I require, plain and simple. Would that pose any problems for you? Please do be as candid as you can."

"Oh, sir, I'm here because I heard that you were an excellent judge to work with. All other concerns are secondary to me at this point, including vacation and, uh, procreation. And I don't know quite how to say this because I don't want to give you the wrong impression." Pausing, Medina spoke in a halting, nervous voice, " I'm not going to get pregnant accidentally, sir, because my . . . uh . . . sexual interests lie more with women, and with my mother to support, I have no intention of using other means to get pregnant at this time."

The judge's face flushed, and he struggled to conceal his surprise, unable to suppress the reflexive thought: "A lesbian, eh? I'd never have guessed, her being so attractive." Never having met a self-identified Haitian lesbian, he experienced a quick succession of thoughts: "How's it going to look when I stand for election and people find out that I had a lesbian clerk? Isn't she going to be biased in all the difficult family law cases that I get? How about that case last term involving the sperm donor who wanted to be declared the father of a child that two lesbians were coparenting?" He made a mental note to talk to some other colleagues about this application, to find out whether they had ever had a homosexual clerk. Eager to conclude the interview, given his upcoming noon fund-raiser for his reelection campaign, but also fully aware that he was not likely to find a more qualified minority clerk and not wanting to seem to be ending things because of her comments about her sexuality, the judge answered, "Uh, your mother. . . . right. Tell you what—I'll get back to you after I interview a few more candidates for the position. Thank you very much for your time. And *give your mother my best wishes. I am sure she must be very proud of you. And don't worry, your sexuality would not be an issue one way or the other as it pertains to—or, rather, doesn't pertain to—the judge smiled—your application."*

Medina never heard from the judge again, and her former clients tell her that they never were called. She suspects that her brief went unread as well. And although she has always been open concerning her lesbianism, she understands that the judge never mentioned it to anyone.

Or could the following be Medina's story?

*Medina attended an American university where she received a full scholarship in recognition of her work on behalf of her family. Helping take care of her ill mother was considered to be important work worthy of recognition. Upon graduation from college, Medina received a stipend from the federal government to work in the community. Accompanying the stipend was a voucher for home health care for her mother who could not stay home by herself all day without assistance. After a few years, Medina decided to attend law school and, once again, received a full scholarship in recognition of her work both in the home and in the community.*

*When a Latino lawyer was elected to an opening in the state supreme court, Medina decided to apply for a clerkship. Once again, she found herself in his chambers, but this time with her hair in corn rows and her favorite colorful scarf wrapped around her head. The judge glanced at her as he came into the interview room. He was looking forward to this interview, having heard that Medina had been a real standout at the local law school. He knew that he might be criticized if he only hired* minority clerks, but Medina was so well qualified that he hoped that he could get away with hiring her.

"Thank you for coming in with so little notice. As I imagine you've figured out from the quick response time, I called you to arrange an interview as soon as your application came across my desk."

"Thank you, sir. I was very flattered by your immediate interest in my candidacy. I hadn't expected to get a call from you directly! When I canvassed for your campaign, I had no idea that I might find myself in your office someday, talking about whether I might be qualified to work with you. It's a real honor to be here."

"So, I see that you supported yourself through college and law school," says the judge. "I, too, had the pleasure of being able to take care of family responsibilities while getting more education."

"Yes," replies Medina, "the Family Partnership Act has made a big difference in my community. We no longer have to choose between taking care of ailing relatives and getting an education. The definition of work has been expanded to include work in the family. My mother can also now receive retirement benefits through Social Security, which gives her credit for the years she spent taking care of us in the home. It is now understood that she had two jobs—taking care of other family's children and taking care of us. And although her employer never contributed to Social Security on her behalf, she recently received a large settlement on behalf of all domestic workers who were coerced into not receiving Social Security benefits. The Bayer family is now on probation for their illegal actions and is reportedly paying Social Security taxes for their current domestic workers."

"I hear that the 'three strikes and you're out' policy has really improved the record of payment for domestic workers. Didn't I also hear that Mr. Bayer was prosecuted for his sexual harassment of your mother?"

"No, the new law protecting domestic workers from sexual harassment wasn't retroactive, but my mother did testify before Congress about her mistreatment. I suspect the publicity from that testimony was sufficient punishment for Mr. Bayer. He was apparently demoted at his job because of his inability to work well with professional women."

"How is your mother's health?"

"The national health insurance program that was instituted has allowed her to receive innovative therapies for people with Alzheimer's. Although she'll never regain the memory she has lost, her rate of deterioration has slowed tremendously. I bet Mr. Bayer wishes her memory would have faded more rapidly!"

"Well, we should talk about your ability as a potential law clerk. I see you have a very fine record in school, but I've learned not to put too much weight on a clerk's grades. Can you give me other evidence of your abilities?"

"My work on behalf of the Haitian Law Student Association might help you. I do volunteer work on behalf of illegal immigrants and recently wrote an amicus brief on a pending Supreme Court case. If you will protect the confidentiality of my clients, I can give you some phone numbers to call to get references. And I can leave a copy of the brief for you to read."

"Thank you. I find that personal references from pro bono clients can be the most useful sort of reference. I will definitely call as many of those people as I can. One of my other clerks can also help if I have any language difficulties. Well, this really *looks like a strong application. Do you have any questions for me?"*

*"Um, I don't know quite how to ask this. And I hope you don't take offense. It's not really a question about the job."*

*"Go ahead. I promise not to take offense unless you, of course, plan to criticize my tie."*

*"Certainly not, a green tie blends in very nicely with a navy blue suit," Medina answered with a broad smile. "Seriously, I have a personal favor to ask of you and didn't know when else I might be able to ask you."*

*"Fire away. The worst I can do is say no."*

*"My partner and I are planning to get married this summer and were wondering if you would officiate at our wedding. As you know, same-sex partners have been able to get lawfully married only since this last year. Elisa is pregnant, and we were hoping to get married before the twins are born."*

*"It would be my pleasure! And if you want to take a leave once the babies are born, please let me know. Our standard practice is to pay 80 percent of your wages for up to six months following the birth of a child. You also have the option of working half-time for up to one year at 80 percent of your normal wages. But when there is a multiple birth, those figures are pushed up to 100 percent. I hope you find that policy reasonable."*

*"Thanks. I'll discuss it with Elisa. I suspect I'll want to stay home full time for the first three months and then go to a half-time schedule for the next six months. Elisa can arrange a similar schedule with her employer so we can probably avoid child care for the crucial first nine months of their lives."*

*"Great. I'll look forward to reading your engagement announcement in the newspaper. Feel free to send out invita-*

*tions, and let me know where you want to conduct the cere-mony."*

*"Thanks, judge. I hope this is the beginning of a long-lasting relationship. I, too, hope to be a judge someday and see this job as giving me invaluable experience."*

Neither scenario is likely to happen, of course. Because we are trained to hide our stereotypes and prejudices, the judge would probably know better than to reveal his concerns about preg-nancy at an interview. But Medina would be foolish to think she entered the interview on a level playing field. Her challenge is to reassure her interviewer by offering answers to the ques-tions that he dared not ask like—are you going to get pregnant, does your Haitian work make you too biased to be a fair clerk, are you a rabble-rouser who is going to be hard to get along with?

The second scenario is unlikely to take place because we are not there yet. But sometimes there are hopeful signs. When I was at the end of my recent pregnancy, I got a call from a law school interested in recruiting me for a new position. When I said that I was pregnant and could not travel at that time, they offered to keep the position open until I could travel. They also offered to take care of my infant while I had the interview. Unlike the traditional American model, they saw my preg-nancy as an occasion for accommodation rather than rejection. Of course, I would be naive to think that their response would have been as generous if I had been applying for a janitorial or secretarial position. (In fact, it was a secretary, not the dean, who took care of my child while I was interviewed.) Only thirty years ago, women were forced to quit their jobs as soon as they became pregnant. Today, they can sometimes interview while visibly or recently pregnant. We can only hope that these advances will become more widespread in our society as we come to better respect the worker and his or her role in the family. American capitalism can and must do better. Our lives depend on it.

# NOTES

**Notes to Chapter 1**

1. George Soros, "The Capitalist Threat," *Atlantic Monthly* 45 (February 1997).

2. Robert Kuttner, *Everything for Sale: The Virtues and Limits of Markets* (1997).

3. Leonard Silk and Mark Silk, with Robert Heilbroner, Jonas Pontusson, and Bernard Wasow, *Making Capitalism Work* (1996).

4. *Id.* at 2 (quoting Dick Armey, the House majority leader).

5. Jules L. Coleman, "Efficiency, Utility, and Wealth Maximization," 8 *Hofstra L. Rev.* 509, 549 (1980).

6. Kuttner, *supra* note 2, at 6.

7. Richard A. Posner, *Economic Analysis of Law* (4th ed., 1992).

8. *Id.* at 17.

9. *Id.* at 465.

10. Maria J. Hanratty, "Social Welfare Programs for Women and

Children: The United States versus France," in Rebecca M. Blank, ed., *Social Protection versus Economic Flexibility* 301 (1994).

11. Siv Gustafsson and Frank P. Stafford, "Three Regimes of Child Care: The United States, the Netherlands, and Sweden," in Blank, ed., *Social Protection versus Economic Flexibility*, 333, 346.

12. David Barnes and Lynn Stout are the authors of a 1992 casebook entitled *Cases and Materials on Law and Economics*. As Posner does, they explore how the economic concepts of efficiency and utility maximization can be applied to law. Their modest improvement over Posner's work is that they end each unit with notes and questions for the students concerning, for example, some of the assumptions made by economists. The scope of the topics they explore is also much more limited than the scope of topics chosen by Posner. They do not, for example, discuss criminal law, although they do consider some aspects of the social welfare state. Again, the approach is entirely parochial with no comparison with the laws of other countries. In addition, their work refers to "public choice theory," a jurisprudential perspective akin to law and economics. No section is directly labeled a "critique"; at most, students might develop a critique from their innovative responses to the questions posed by the authors at the end of each unit. Similarly, *An Introduction to Law and Economics* by A. Mitchell Polinsky (a 150-page paperback published in 1992), and *Law and Economics* by Robert Cooter and Thomas Ulen (a 644-page hardbound textbook published in 1988), proceed from the unexamined assumption that the legal system should be based on economic principles.

13. Robert Cooter and Thomas Ulen, preface to *Law and Economics* (1988).

14. See, e.g., City of Richmond v. J. A. Croson Co., 488 U.S. 469, 528 (1989) (Scalia, J., concurring).

15. Johnson v. Transportation Agency, 480 U.S. 616, 677 (1987) (Scalia, J., dissenting).

16. See United States v. Virginia, 116 S.Ct. 2274 (1996).

17. See Johnson v. Transportation Agency, 480 U.S. 616 (1987).

18. Kumpf v. Steinhaus, 779 F.2d 1323, 1326 (7th Cir. 1985).

19. Barbara Bennett Woodhouse, "A Public Role in the Private

Family: The Parental Rights and Responsibilities Act and the Politics of Child Protection and Education," 57 *Ohio St. L.J.* 393, 421, note 88 (1996).

20. Ann Shola Orloff, "Gender and the Social Rights of Citizenship: The Comparative Analysis of Gender Relations and Welfare States," 58 *American Sociological Review* 303, 323 (1993).

21. See Adam Smith, *The Wealth of Nations* (1964) (originally published in 1776). For other descriptions of classical laissez-faire economics, see David Ricardo, *The Principles of Political Economy and Taxation* (1963) (originally published in 1817); and John Stuart Mill, *Principles of Political Economy* (1970) (originally published in 1848).

22. William J. Baumol, *Microtheory: Applications and Origins* 245 (1986).

23. Thomas Earl Geu and Martha S. Davis, "Work: A Legal Analysis in the Context of the Changing Transnational Political Economy," 63 *U. Cin. L. Rev.* 1679, 1688 (1995).

24. John Maynard Keynes, *The General Theory of Employment, Interest, and Money* 13 (1964) (originally published in 1936).

25. Rebecca M. Blank, introduction to Rebecca M. Blank, ed., *Social Protection versus Economic Stability* 12 (1994).

26. Jonas Pontusson, "Wither Northern Europe?" in Silk, *supra* note 3, at 128.

27. Alan Enrehalt, "Keepers of the Dismal Faith," *New York Times* E13 (Feb. 23, 1997).

### Notes to Chapter 2

1. Patricia Williams, "The Pathology of Privilege," *Women's Review of Books* 1 (May 1996).

2. John D. Lamb, "The Real Affirmative Action Babies: Legacy Preferences at Harvard and Yale," 26 *Colum. J.L. & Soc. Probs.* 491, 492–93 (1993).

3. Stephanie M. Wildman, *Privilege Revealed: How Invisible Preference Undermines America* 10 (1996).

4. Michael Lind, *The Next American Nation: The New Nationalism and the Fourth American Revolution* 169 (1995).

5. Michael Selmi, "Testing for Equality: Merit, Efficiency, and the Affirmative Action Debate," 42 *U.C.L.A. L. Rev.* 1251, 1251–52 (1995). For the view that "elitism" is becoming less fashionable, see William A. Henry III, *In Defense of Elitism* (1994).

6. Williams, *supra* note 1, at 1.

7. Richard A. Posner, "The DeFunis Case and the Constitutionality of Preferential Treatment of Racial Minorities," *Sup. Ct. Rev.* 1, 18 (1974).

8. Richard Epstein, *Forbidden Grounds* 413 (1992).

9. Posner, *supra* note 7, at 18.

10. *Id.* at 11.

11. Lamb, *supra* note 2, at 495–96.

12. *Id.* at 501.

13. Anthony J. Scanlon, "The History and Culture of Affirmative Action," 1988 *B.Y.U.L. Rev.* 343, 354 (1988).

14. Edward J. Littlejohn and Leonard S. Rubinowitz, "Black Enrollment in Law Schools: Forward to the Past?" 12 *Thurgood Marshall L. Rev.* 415, 427 (1987).

15. Scanlon, *supra* note 13, at 352.

16. See Jeffrey Owings, Marilyn McMillen, and John Burkett, "Making the Cut: Who Meets Highly Selective College Entrance Criteria," National Center for Education Statistics, U.S. Department of Education, Office of Educational Research and Improvement (April 1995) at 4 (table 1).

17. Lamb, *supra* note 2, at 492–93.

18. David E. Van Zandt, "Merit at the Right Tail: Education and Elite Law School Admissions," 64 *Tex. L. Rev.* 1493, 1515 (1986).

19. Derrick A. Bell Jr., "Preferential Affirmative Action," 16 *Harv. C.R.–C.L. L. Rev.* 855, 865 (1982).

20. John K. Wilson, *The Myth of Political Correctness* 149 (1995).

21. Scanlon, *supra* note 13, at 354.

22. 78 F.3d 932 (5th Cir. 1995).

23. Sweatt v. Painter, 339 U.S. 629 (1950).

24. 78 F.3d 932 (5th Cir. 1995).

25. *Id.* at 946, citing Richard A. Posner, "The DeFunis Case and the Constitutionality of Preferential Treatment of Racial Minorities," 1974 *Sup. Ct. Rev.* 1, 12 (1974).

26. Randall Kennedy, "Persuasion and Distrust: A Comment on the Affirmative Action Debate," 99 *Harv. L. Rev.* 1327, 1330 (1986).

27. *Id.* at 1331.

28. Lind, *supra* note 4, at 331.

29. John Larew, "Why Are Droves of Unqualified, Unprepared Kids Getting into Our Top Colleges? Because Their Dads Are Alumni," *Washington Monthly* (June 1991).

30. *Id.*

31. Wilson, *supra* note 20, at 151.

32. Selmi, *supra* note 5, at 1262.

33. Thomas A. Cunniff, "The Price of Equal Opportunity: The Efficiency of Title VII after Hicks," 45 *Case W. Res. L. Rev.* 507, 535–56 (1995).

34. Epstein, *supra* note 8, at 214.

35. Aguilera v. Cook County Police and Corrections Merit Board, 760 F.2d 844 (7th Cir.1985).

36. See e.g., Freeman v. City of Philadelphia, 751 F. Supp. 509 (E.D. Pa. 1990); Officers for Justice v. Civil Service Comm'n, 473 F. Supp. 801 (W.D. Calif. 1979); Vanguard Justice Society v. Hughes, 471 F. Supp. 670 (D. Md. 1979).

37. Kennedy, *supra* note 26, at 1332–33 (quoting Prof. Wasserstrom).

38. Daniel R. Hansen, "Do We Need the Bar Examination? A Critical Evaluation of the Justification for the Bar Examination and Proposed Alternatives," 45 *Case W. Res. L. Rev.* 1191, 1195 (1995).

39. See generally Deborah L. Rhode and David Luban, *Legal Ethics* 67–71 (1995).

40. Jerold S. Auerbach, *Unequal Justice* 1197–98 (1976).

41. *Id.* at 1199.

42. Lind, *supra* note 4, at 153. See also Manuel R. Ramos, "Legal Malpractice: No Lawyer or Client Is Safe," 47 *Fla. L. Rev.* 1 (1995).

43. Richardson v. McFadden, 540 F.2d 744, 747 (1976).

44. Auerbach, *supra* note 40, at 294.

45. *Id.* at 1206.

46. Richardson, 540 F.2d at 749.

47. *Id.* at 750.

48. 401 U.S. 424 (1971).

49. This is a higher standard than was employed in the Fourth Circuit's bar examination case. See Richardson, 540 F.2d at 748 ("under the Equal Protection Clause of the Fourteenth Amendment the issue is still whether the examination is job related, albeit a less demanding inquiry [than under Title VII]").

50. Epstein, *supra* note 8, at 215.

51. *Id.* at 236.

52. *Id.* at 215.

53. United States v. Georgia Power, 474 F.2d 906, 925 (5th Cir. 1973).

54. Jonathan Tilove, "White 'Legacies' vs. Affirmative Action," *Arizona Republic* (April 9, 1995).

55. Alfred W. Blumrosen, "The Duty of Fair Recruitment under the Civil Rights Act of 1964," 22 *Rutgers L. Rev.* 465, 481 (1868).

56. 947 F.2d 292 (7th Cir. 1991).

57. 989 F.2d 233 (7th Cir. 1993).

58. EEOC v. O&G Spring and Wire Forms Speciality Co., 38 F.3d 872, 888 (7th Cir. 1994).

59. EEOC v. O&G Spring and Wire Forms Speciality Co., 705 F. Supp. 400, 403 (N.D. Ill. 1988).

60. 38 F.3d at 893.

61. See James Bovard, "The Latest EEOC Quota Madness," *Wall Street Journal* A14 (April 27, 1995).

62. See Re Mac Vicar and Superintendent of Family & Child Services et al., 34 D.L.R. (4th) 488 (B.C.S.C. 1986).

63. See, e.g., Action Travail des Femmes v. Canadian National Railway Co., 40 D.L.R. (4th) 193 (1987) (upholding affirmative action program for female railway workers); Weatherall v. Canada (Attorney-General), 73 D.L.R. (4th) 57 (Federal Ct. of Appeal 1990) (upholding affirmative action plan for female prison guards).

64. 135 D.L.R. 4th 707, 1996 Ont. C.J. LEXIS 2129 (Ontario Court (General Division) 1996).

### Notes to Chapter 3

1. James Bovard, "The Disabilities Act's Parade of Absurdities," *Wall Street Journal* A16 (June 22, 1995).

2. Weaver v. City of Topeka, No. 93–4213-SAC, 1993 U.S. Dist. LEXIS 18586, *4 (D. Kan. Dec. 21, 1993) (In granting a motion to dismiss, the court said: "The court finds nothing in the definition or the proscriptive terms of the Act which could support such a broad reading.")

3. Burns v. Stafford Bd. of Educ., No. CV 93 53581 S. 1995 Conn. Super. LEXIS 1650 at *4 (Conn. Super. Ct. June 2, 1995).

4. Stephanie N. Mehta, "Big Conference Will Feature Eye-Catching Proposals: Topics Range from Enshrining English Language to Killing Disabilities Act," *Wall Street Journal* B2 (June 12, 1995).

5. Debra J. Saunders, editorial, "Free the Berkeley Three," *San Francisco Chronicle*, July 27, 1994.

6. Richard Epstein, *Forbidden Grounds: The Case against Employment Discrimination Laws* 484 (1992).

7. *Id.* at 8.

8. See, e.g., Adarand Constructors, Inc. v. Pena, 115 S. Ct. 2097 (1995); Shaw v. Reno, 113 S. Ct. 2816 (1993) (extending reverse discrimination theory to voting rights cases); City of Richmond v. J. A. Croson Co., 488 U.S. 469 (1989).

9. City of Richmond v. J.A. Croson Co., 488 U.S. 469, 528–29 (Marshall, Brennan, and Blackmun, 5 dissenting).

10. Brian Doyle, *Disability Discrimination and Equal Opportunities: A Comparative Study of the Employment Rights of Disabled Persons* 245–46 (1995).

11. 480 U.S. 616 (1987).

12. Doyle, *supra* note 10, at 221.

13. See, e.g., Berkman v. City of New York, 812 F.2d 52 (2d Cir. 1987).

14. For example, in *Wygant v. Jackson Board of Education,* 476 U.S. 267 (1986), the employer and union decided to protect the employability of African American teachers by not using strict seniority rules that reflected prior discrimination. They thus attempted to modify workplace rules that were not necessary to the efficient operation of the school district.

15. 401 U.S. 424 (1971).

16. Compare 42 U.S.C. § 703(k)(1)(A)(I)(1994) (requiring demonstration "that the challenged practice is job related for the position in question and consistent with business necessity") with 42 U.S.C. § 12113(a)(1994) (requiring demonstration that the challenged practice is "job-related and consistent with business necessity, and such performance cannot be accomplished by reasonable accommodation").

17. 438 U.S. 265 (1978).

18. See, e.g., Trans World Airlines, Inc. v. Hardison, 432 U.S. 63 (1977).

19. See Ruth Colker, "Whores, Fags, Dumb Ass Women, Surly Blacks, and Competent Heterosexual White Men: The Sexual and Racial Morality Underlying Anti-Discrimination Doctrine," 7 *Yale J.L. & Feminism* 195 (1995).

20. Epstein, *supra* note 6, at 419.

21. See generally Ruth Colker, "Anti-Subordination above All: Sex, Race, and Equal Protection," 61 *N.Y.U. L. Rev.* 1003 (1986).

22. See McDonald v. Santa Fe Trail Transp. Co., 427 U.S. 273 (1976).

23. 56 F.3d 695 (5th Cir. 1995).

24. 906 F. Supp. 1561 (S.D. Ga. 1995).

25. *Id,* at 1577, quoting Pedigo v. P.A.M. Transport, Inc., 891 F. Supp. 482, 485–86 (W.D. Ark. 1994) (footnote omitted).

26. 891 F. Supp. 482 (W.D. Ark. 1994).

27. *Id.* at 486.

28. 36 F.3d 939 (10th Cir. 1994).

29. See, e.g., Jasany v. United States Postal Service, 755 F.2d 1244 (6th Cir. 1985) (postal worker); Chandler v. City of Dallas, 2 F.3d 1385

(5th Cir. 1993) (city employee); Elstner v. Southwestern Bell Telephone Co., 863 F.2d 881 (5th Cir. 1988) (service technician).

30. See, e.g., Bombrys v. City of Toledo, 849 F. Supp. 1210 (N.D. Oh. 1993) (police officer requesting permission to carry food or glucose gel or tablets on his person, as well as a penlike device containing an insulin injection kit).

31. See, e.g., Deckert v. City of Ulysses, No. 93–1295-PFK, 1995 WL 580074 (D. Kan. Sept. 6, 1995); Coghlan v. H. J. Heinz Co., 851 F. Supp. 808 (N.D. Tex. 1994).

32. Deckert, 1995 WL 580074.

33. Canadian Human Rights Act, R.S.C., ch. H–6, § 16 (1993) (Can.).

34. See generally Roberts v. Ontario, 117 D.L.R. 4th 297 (1994).

35. See generally Ontario (Human Rights Commission) v. Etobicoke (Borough), 132 D.L.R. (3d) 14, 22–23 (1982) (requiring multifactor analysis to determine whether mandatory retirement can be imposed on firefighters below the age of sixty-five); Re Ontario (Human Rights Commission) and Simpson-Sears, 23 D.L.R. (4th) 321, 335 (1985) (implying a duty "to take steps to accommodate the complainant, short of undue hardship" in religious discrimination case; placing the burden of proof on employer to demonstrate undue hardship); Re Embrick Plastics Div. of Windsor Mold Inc. and Ontario Human Rights Comm'n, 90 D.L.R. (4th) 476 (1992) (requiring employer to accommodate pregnant woman who could not safely work in the spray-painting area).

36. Doyle, *supra* note 10, at 228.

37. 42 L.A.C. 4th 86 (1994).

38. Human Rights Code, S.M. 1987–88, c. 45 (C.C.S.M., c. H175).

39. See, e.g., Babcock and Wilcox Industries Ltd. and U.S.W.A., 42 L.A.C. 4th 209 (1994) (ruling that the griever, who was an alcoholic, should be "put back into the employer's place of work to resume his duties" once the physician certifies that the griever is "fit to return to work"); Re Canada Post Corp. and Canadian Union of Postal Workers, 38 L.A.C. 4th 1 (1993) (ruling that the employer has obligation to assign the griever to a vacancy in another mail unit that would not involve heavy lifting); Re United Air Lines and International Associa-

tion of Machinists & Aerospace Workers, 33 L.A.C. 4th 89 (1993) (reinstatement with modified work conditions order following head injury to employee).

40. Ontario Human Rights Code, 10(1).

41. Canadian Human Rights Act, R.S.C. 1985, c. H-6 (as amended), s. 25.

42. Re Canadian National Railway Co. and C.A.W.-Canada, 43 L.A.C. 4th 129 (1994).

43. Re Babcock and Wilcox Industries Ltd. and U.S.W.A., Loc. 2859, 42 L.A.C. 4th 209 (1994).

44. See Disabled Person (Employment) Act 1994 (c 10) (1 March 1944) (Great Britain). "This section is prospectively repealed by the Disability Discrimination Act 1995, ss 61(7), 70(5), Sch. 7, as from a day to be appointed." (LEXIS Annotation).

45. Jamal v. Secretary, Department of Health, 14 NSWLR 14 (1988).

46. See, e.g., Scott & Anor v. Telstra Corporation Limited ¶ 92–717 (Human Rights and Equal Opportunity Commission ruling) (requiring the employer to provide teletypewriters to profoundly hearing impaired employees). See generally Bonnie Poitras Tucker, "The Disability Discrimination Act: Ensuring Rights of Australians with Disabilities, Particularly Hearing Impairments," 21 *Monash Univ. L. Rev.* 15, 26, note 74 (1995) (describing several cases under the Australian state disability discrimination law in which the plaintiffs prevailed by demonstrating a failure to reasonably accommodate their disabilities).

47. Disability Discrimination Act of 1992, 1992 Aust. Act § 135(4) (1995).

48. See, e.g., Archibald v. Commissioner, NSW Fire Brigades ¶ 92–736 (ruling by Equal Opportunity Tribunal in New South Wales) (complainant who had reconstructive surgery on both his knees was a person with a disability).

### Notes to Chapter 4

1. Troupe v. May Department Stores, 20 F.3d 734 (7th Cir. 1994).
2. See, e.g., General Electric Co. v. Gilbert, 429 U.S. 125 (1976).

3. See Brooks v. Canada Safeway, Ltd., 59 D.L.R. 4th 321 (1989) (a disability benefit plan that denied benefits to a pregnant women was found to violate the sex-equality principle).

4. Pregnancy Discrimination Act, Pub. L. No. 95–555, 95 Stat. 2076 (1978) (codified at 42 U.S.C. § 2000e(k)(1988)). The PDA states: "The terms 'because of sex' or 'on the basis of sex' include, but are not limited to, because of or on the basis of pregnancy, childbirth, or related medical conditions; and women affected by pregnancy, childbirth, or related medical conditions shall be treated the same for all employment-related purposes, including receipt of benefits under fringe benefit programs, as other persons not so affected but similar in their ability or inability to work." 42 U.S.C. §2000e(k).

5. See, e.g., Troupe v. May Department Stores, 20 F.3d 734 (7th Cir. 1994) (the plaintiff lost because she could not produce comparative evidence of a man who had had tardiness problems before a period of scheduled leave was to commence).

6. See, e.g., Schafer v. Board of Education, 903 F.2d 243 (3rd Cir. 1990) (a collective-bargaining agreement that permitted a woman to take up to one year of leave following the birth of a child violated the PDA because the leave was not available to men).

7. Occupational Safety and Health Act of 1970, 29 U.S.C. § 654(a)(1)(general duty clause).

8. See Carol Daugherty Rasnic, "The United States' 1993 Family and Medical Leave Act: How Does It Compare with Work Leave Laws in European Countries?" 10 *Conn. J. Int'l L.* 105, 105 (1994).

9. Family and Medical Leave Act of 1993, Pub. L. No. 103–3 (H.R. 1), 107 Stat. 6, 29 U.S.C. §2601 (1993).

10. Richard Epstein, *Forbidden Grounds* 329, 349 (1992)

11. See Rasnic, *supra* note 8, at 142.

12. See, e.g., Martin H. Malin, "Fathers and Parental Leave," 72 *Tex. L. Rev.* 1047 (1994).

13. See generally Edward F. Zigler and Mary E. Lang, *Child Care Choices: Balancing the Needs of Children, Family and Society* 83 (1991) (reporting Jay Belsky's research that "infants who experience more than twenty hours per week of supplementary child care in the

first year of life are at risk of developing insecure attachments and later social-emotional problems"); Alison Clarke-Stewart, *Daycare* 116–121 (rev. ed., 1993) (surveys the literature on whether infants should be in day care at all); Mackenzie Carpenter, "U.S. Lags on Parental Leave Policy," *Pittsburgh Post-Gazette* (June 3, 1996) ("Most experts say that the best thing for children would be for parents to remain home with them for the first four to six months. Others say a year would be better.")

14. Epstein, *supra* note 10, at 334–40.

15. *Id.* at 329.

16. Joanne S. Lublin, "Family-Leave Law Can Be Excuse for a Day Off," *Wall Street Journal* (July 7, 1995). See also Editorial, "Taking Leave," *Wall Street Journal* (April 17, 1995); Gary Klotz, "Regulatory Chokehold: The High Cost of 'Employees' Rights," *Wall Street Journal* (Aug. 3, 1993).

17. Richard A. Posner, "An Economic Analysis of Sex Discrimination Laws," 56 *U. Chi. L. Rev.* 1311, 1332 (1989).

18. *Id.* at 1313.

19. 886 F.2d 871, 902 (7th Cir. 1988) (Posner, C.J., dissenting).

20. Irving S. Michelman, *The Moral Limitations of Capitalism* 15 (1994).

21. 886 F.2d at 902.

22. Samuel Issacharoff and Elyse Rosenblum, "Women and the Workplace: Accommodating the Demands of Pregnancy," 94 *Columbia L. Rev.* 2154 (1994). See also Mikel A. Glavinovich, "International Suggestions for Improving Parental Leave Legislation in the United States," 13 *Ariz. J. Int'l & Comp. Law* 147 (1996) (offering economic arguments for mandating adequate parental leave).

23. See Facts on File, *The New Book of World Rankings* (3d ed., 1991).

24. See generally Facts on File, *World News Digest Facts on File* (Feb. 11, 1993), 1993 WL 2524600.

25. See Unemployment Insurance Act, as amended, chap. U-1, s. 20 (1990). Each province also has its own statute governing unemployment insurance for maternity and parenting leave.

26. See act to amend the Employment Standards Act with respect to Pregnancy and Parental Leave, R.S.O. ch. 26, § 38(1) (1991).

27. For an excellent description of Italian law, see Paolo Wright-Carozza, "Organic Goods: Legal Understandings of Work, Parenthood, and Gender Equality in Comparative Perspective," 81 *Calif. L. Rev.* 531, 542–48 (1993).

28. *Id.* at 551–52 (quoting Judgment of July 15, 1991, Corte cost., 114 Foro it. I 2298 (1991). The Canadian courts have similarly extended benefits to fathers on equality grounds. See Schachter v. Canada, 93 D.L.R. 4th 1 (1992).

29. See Rasnic, *supra* note 8, at 113–135 (summarizing the European situation).

30. Nickie McWhirter, "Good, Bad News on Family Leave Act," *Detroit News* (May 11, 1996).

31. Carpenter, *supra* note 13.

32. 939 F.2d 440 (7th Cir. 1991).

33. *Id.* at 445.

34. Re Ontario Secondary School Teachers' Federation, District 34 and Barton et al., 136 D.L.R.4th 34 (1996).

35. See, e.g., Re Belleville General Hospital and Services Employees Union, Local 183, 37 L.A.C. 4th 375 (1993) (court deferring to the judgment of the employee's physician despite his extensive history of absenteeism in violation of company policy).

36. *Id.*

37. See ADA Title I Interpretive Guidance, 29 CFR § 1630.2(I) Appendix ("other conditions, such as pregnancy, that are not the result of a physiological disorder are also not impairments"). Courts have generally followed these ADA guidelines. See, e.g., Gudenkauf v. Stauffer Communications, Inc., 922 F. Supp. 465 (D. Kansas 1996) (a woman experiencing a normal pregnancy cannot use the FMLA to request leave during her pregnancy). But see Deborah A. Calloway, "Accommodating Pregnancy in the Workplace," 25 *Stetson L. Rev.* 1 (1995) (arguing that the ADA should be applied to pregnant women seeking accommodations at the workplace).

38. Connecticut General Statutes, section 46a–60(a)(7)(E).

39. Fenn Manufacturing v. Commission on Human Rights and Opportunities, No. CIV. CV 92–509435, 1994 WL 51143 at *20 (Conn. Super. 1994).

40. 20 F.3d 734 (7th Cir. 1994).

41. See Ann C. McGinley and Jeffrey W. Stempel, "Condescending Contradictions: Richard Posner's Pragmatism and Pregnancy Discrimination," 46 *Fla. L. Rev.* 193, 213 (1994).

42. Posner, *supra* note 17, at 1315.

43. The mixed-motives theory was developed in Price Waterhouse v. Hopkins, 490 U.S. 228, 244–45 (1989) and later modified by the Civil Rights Act of 1991, Pub. L. No. 102–166, sec. 107(a), 105 Stat. 1071, 1075 (1991) (codified at 42 U.S.C. §2000e–2(m)). Because the 1991 Civil Rights Act did not apply to Troupe's case, the standard from Price Waterhouse applied—that defendants in mixed-motive cases can be absolved of liability by showing that they would have made the same decision even if impermissible discrimination had not occurred.

44. The district court judge considered but rejected the applicability of a mixed-motives theory. See Troupe v. May Department Stores, No. 92–C2605, 1993 U.S. Dist. LEXIS 7751, at *7 (N.D. Ill. June 3, 1993).

45. 90 D.L.R. 4th 476 (Ontario Court, Divisional Court 1992).

46. See Canadian Human Rights Act, c. 33, § 3(2).

47. 29 L.A.C. 4th 202 (1992).

48. 479 U.S. 272 (1987).

49. The case was technically a supremacy clause case, which means that the Court had to determine whether it was possible to comply with both the PDA and state law.

50. 479 U.S. at 290.

51. California Federal Savings and Loan Association v. Guerra, 758 F.2d 390, 392 (9th Cir. 1985).

52. 90 D.L.R. 4th 703 (Alberta Court of Queen's Bench 1992).

53. 741 F.2d 444 (D.C. Cir. 1984).

54. 29 U.S.C. § 654(a)(1)(1982).

55. 499 U.S. 187 (1991).

56. See Nadine Taub, "At the Intersection of Reproductive Freedom

and Gender Equality: Problems in Addressing Reproductive Hazards in the Workplace," 6 *UCLA Women's L.J.* 443, 451 (1996). The United States' solution to the problem of reproductive hazards is also unthinkable in Germany. See generally Carol D. Rasnic, "Germany's Legal Protection for Women Workers vis-à-vis Illegal Employment Discrimination in the United States: A Comparative Perspective in Light of Johnson Controls," 13 *Mich. J. Int'l L.* 415 (1992).

57. See Council Directive 92/85, art. 5, 1992 O.J. (L348), as cited in Marley S. Weiss, "The Impact of the European Community on Labor Law: Some American Comparisons," 68 *Chicago-Kent L. Rev.* 1427, 1467, note 94 (1993).

58. See EEOC v. Detroit-Macomb Hospital Corp., 952 F.2d 403 (6th Cir. 1992) (table, text in Westlaw, No. 91–1088, 91–1278). See also Armstrong v. Flowers Hospital, Inc., 812 F. Supp. 1183 (M.D. Ala. 1993) (a pregnant woman with gestational diabetes was fired after she refused to treat a patient with cryptococcal meningitis, an opportunistic infection likely to be more dangerous to a fetus *in utero* than to a healthy adult); Sanderson v. St. Louis University, 586 F. Supp. 954 (E.D. Mo. 1984) (a pregnant security officer was denied a request for light duty work during her pregnancy).

59. Armstrong v. Flowers, 33 F.3d 1308, 1314 (11th Cir. 1994).

60. See, e.g., Hunt-Golliday v. Metropolitan Water Reclamation District of Greater Chicago, 14 A.D.D. 100 (N.D. Ill. 1996) (a pregnant woman was fired after she complained of stomach cramps when lifting heavy objects).

61. See, e.g., Jackson v. Veterans Administration, 22 F.3d 277 (11th Cir. 1994) (not being absent is an essential job function; an employee with excessive absenteeism is therefore not an a "qualified individual with a disability" under federal law).

62. See, e.g., Re Hamilton Street Railway Co. and Amalgamated Transit Union, Local 107, 41 L.A.C. 4th 1 (1994) (the griever missed work nearly half of the year over a period of several years yet was considered to be a qualified individual with a disability under the law of Ontario); Re Toronto Hospital and Ontario Nurses' Association, 31 L.A.C. 4th 44 (1992) (the griever prevailed in a case involving exces-

sive absenteeism due to a disability). See also Re Canadian National Railway Co. and Niles et al., 94 D.L.R. 4th (Fed. Ct. of Appeal 1992) (an employee's absenteeism was found to be a lawful basis for discharge only because the court found that the employee did not offer sufficient evidence of rehabilitation from his condition of alcoholism).

63. See ADA Title I Interpretive Guidance, 29 CFR § 1630.2(I) Appendix ("other conditions, such as pregnancy, that are not the result of a physiological disorder are also not impairments"). Courts have generally followed these ADA guidelines. See, e.g., Gudenkauf v. Stauffer Communications, Inc., 922 F. Supp. 465 (D. Kansas 1996) (a woman experiencing a normal pregnancy cannot use the FMLA to request leave during her pregnancy). But see Calloway, *supra* note 37 (arguing that ADA should be applied to pregnant women seeking accommodations at the workplace).

64. See Ruth Colker, *Pregnant Men: Practice, Theory and the Law* (1994).

65. 29 U.S.C. §§ 2601–2654 (1995).

66. An eligible employee "means an employee who has been employed (1) for at least 12 months by the employer with respect to whom leave is requested...and (2) for at least 1,250 hours of service with such employer during the previous 12-month period" 29 U.S.C. §2611(2).

67. The term *employer* "means any person engaged in commerce or in any industry or activity affecting commerce who employs 50 or more employees for each working day during each of 20 or more calendar workweeks in the current or preceding calendar years"; 29 U.S.C. §2611(4)(a).

68. 29 CFR §825.114(a)(1996).

69. Marcus D. Ward, "The Family and Medical Leave Act of 1993: A Sound Investment, or an Expensive Lesson in Employee Benefits?" 20 *T. Marshall L. Rev.* 413, 422 (1995).

70. Mona L. Schuchmann, "The Family and Medical Leave Act of 1993: A Comparative Analysis with Germany," 20 *J. Corp. L.* 331 (1995).

71. See "Hard Line in Germany on Work Benefits," *New York Times* C3 (Oct. 1, 1996).

72. S. Rep. No. 3, 103d Cong., 1st sess. 1993, 1993 U.S.C.C.A. . 3, at pp. 30–31.

73. 29 C.F.R. §§825.114(a)(2)(ii); 825.800.

74. Gudenkauf v. Stauffer Communications, Inc., 922 F. Supp. 465 (D. Kansas 1996).

75. See, e.g., Brown v. J.C. Penney Corporation, 924 F. Supp. 1158 (S.D. Fla. 1996) (the plaintiff was not covered by FMLA for absence from work following the death of her father).

76. Brannon v. OshKosh B'Gosh, 897 F. Supp. 1028 (D. Tenn. 1995).

77. See Hott v. VDO Yazaki Corporation, 922 F. Supp. 1114 (W.D. Va. 1996).

78. See Seidle v. Provident Mutual Life Insurance Company, 871 F. Supp. 238 (E.D. Pa. 1994).

79. See Oswalt v. Sara Lee Corp., 889 F. Supp. 253 (N.D. Miss. 1995).

80. See *New York Times* A1 (Sept. 12, 1996).

81. See also Freemon v. Foley, 911 F. Supp. 326 (N.D. Illinois 1995) (the plaintiff was discharged after she failed to provide sufficient documentation concerning her children's chicken pox).

82. See also George v. Associated Stationers, 1996 WL 406169 (N.D. Ohio June 3, 1996) (the plaintiff used hospital emergency room to diagnose and treat his chicken pox several days after becoming ill).

83. Compare George v. Associated Stationers, 1996 WL 406169 (N.D. Ohio June 3, 1996) with Seidle v. Provident Mutual Life Insurance Company, 871 F. Supp. 238 (E.D. Pa. 1994).

84. Bauer v. Dayton-Walther Corporation, 910 F. Supp. 306 (E.D. Ky 1996).

85. Day v. Excel Corporation, 1996 WL 294341 (D. Kan. May 17, 1996).

86. Tuberville v. Personal Finance Corporation, 1996 WL 407571 (June 5, 1996).

87. See *New York Times* C3 (Oct. 1, 1996).

88. See Re Bell Canada and Communications, Energy & Paperworkers Union of Canada, 53 L.A.C. 4th 228 (1996).

89. See Rasnic, *supra* note 8.

90. See Jane Rigler, "Analysis and Understanding of the Family and Medical Leave Act of 1993," 45 *Case W. Res. L. Rev.* 457 (1995).

91. H.R. 2020, Parental and Disability Leave Act of 1985 (April 4, 1985).

92. H.R. 925, Reported out of House Committee on Education and Labor by a roll call vote of 21 to 11 (Nov. 17, 1987).

93. S.345, Family and Medical Leave Act of 1989 (Feb. 2, 1989).

94. H.R. 770, 101st Cong., 2d sess. (May 10, 1990).

95. President Bush vetoed the bill on June 29, 1990, and again on September 22, 1992. See generally Donna Lenhoff and Claudia Withers, "Implementation of the Family and Medical Leave Act: Toward the Family-Friendly Workplace," 3 *Am. U.J. Gender & L.* 39, 64 (1994).

96. President Clinton signed the bill on February 5, 1993. S. 5, Family and Medical Leave Act of 1993, 103d Cong., 1st sess. (1993).

97. See H.R. 103–8(II) (Feb. 2, 1993). See also Hearing before the Subcommittee on Children, Family, Drugs and Alcoholism of the Committee on Labor and Human Resources, S.5, 102d Cong., 1st sess. (Jan. 24, 1991) (includes testimony of Dr. Berry Brazelton).

98. Legislative Hearing on H.R.1, the Family and Medical Leave Act, Hearing before the Subcommittee on Labor-Management Relations of the Committee on Education and Labor, 103rd Cong., 1st sess. (Jan. 26, 1993) at 27.

99. 29 U.S.C. § 2612(e)(2)(B).

100. Manual v. Westlake Polymers Corporation, 66 F.3d 758, 764 (5th Cir. 1995).

101. See also Hendry v. GTE North, Inc., 896 F. Supp. 816 (N.D. Indiana 1995) (the employee was found not to have to comply strictly with notice requirements under FMLA because the employer did not properly post information about FMLA at the workplace).

102. Johnson v. Primerica, 1996 WL 34148 at *1 (S.D. N.Y. January 30, 1996).

103. See generally Fry v. First Fidelity Bancorporation, 1996 WL 36910 (E.D. Pa. 1996).

104. Phoebe H. Cottingham, introduction to Phoebe H. Cottingham and David T. Ellwood, eds., *Welfare Policy for the 1990s* 2 (1989).

105. Douglas J. Besharov, "Targeting Long-Term Welfare Recipients in Welfare Policy for the 1990s," in Cottingham and Ellwood, eds., *Welfare Policy for the 1990s* 161.

106. Personal Responsibility and Work Opportunity Reconciliation Act of 1996, Public Law 104–193, section 401(b) (Aug. 21, 1996).

107. As of January 1, 1987, France provided the following benefits to families:

1. A family allowance program for families with two or more children; assistance is not means tested.
2. A family support allowance to children with an absent parent; assistance is not means tested.
3. A parental education allowance for parents of three or more children; some eligibility requirements exist.
4. An allowance for young children that is partly means tested. The program continues until the youngest child reaches age three.
5. A large-family supplement for families with three or more children, all over the age of three; this is means tested.
6. A return-to-school allowance for each child aged six through sixteen who is registered to attend school; this is means tested.
7. A single-parent allowance; this is means tested.
8. A housing allowance to low-income households with a dependent child.

Maria J. Hanratty, "Social Welfare Programs for Women and Children: The United States versus France," in Maria J. Hanratty, *Social Protection versus Economic Flexibility* 326–27 (1994).

108. Since 1980, Sweden has instituted "daddy days," which are leave periods reserved exclusively for fathers to encourage them to participate more fully in child care. Siv Gustafsson and Frank P. Stafford, *Three Regimes of Child Care: The United States, the Netherlands, and Sweden in Social Protection versus Economic Flexibility* 343 (1994).

**Notes to Chapter 5**

1. See generally Watkins v. United States Army, 551 F. Supp. 212 (W.D. Wash. 1982).

2. Watkins v. United States Army, 837 F.2d 1428, 1430 (9th Cir. 1988).

3. Mary Ann Humphrey, "Perry Watkins," in Mary Ann Humphrey, *My Country, My Right to Serve* (1988), reprinted in William B. Rubenstein, *Cases and Materials on Sexual Orientation and the Law* 649 (1997).

4. Watkins v. United States Army, 837 F.2d 1428, 1430 (9th Cir. 1988).

5. Watkins v. United States Army, 551 F. Supp. 212, 223 (W.D. Wash. 1982).

6. See generally Peter Irons, "Interview with Michael Hardwick," reprinted in William B. Rubenstein, *Cases and Materials on Sexual Orientation and the Law* 217–225 (1996).

7. See generally W v. G, 1996 NSW Lexis 2458 (Supreme Court of New South Wales, Feb. 2, 1996).

8. The cases in the United States have generally involved situations in which the second parent seeks visitation rights following the dissolution of the adult relationship. The lesbian coparent has lost in virtually all these cases. See, e.g., Alison D. v. Virginia M., 77 N.Y.2d 651, 569 N.Y.S.2d 586, 572 N.E.2d 27 (1991).

9. Douglas v. The Queen, 98 D.L.R. 4th 129 (Federal Court, Trial Division, Dec. 1, 1992).

10. 94 D.L.R.(4th) 1 (1992).

11. 478 U.S. 186 (1986).

12. Watkins v. United States Army, 847 F.2d 1329, 1353 (9th Cir. 1988) (Reinhardt, C. J., dissenting).

13. Edwin Amenta and Theda Skocpol, "Redefining the New Deal: World War II and the Development of Social Provision in the United States," in Margaret Weir, Ann Shola Orloff, and Theda Skocpol, eds., *The Politics of Social Policy in the United States* 94 (1988).

14. *Id.* at 122.

15. Leonard Silk and Mark Silk, *Making Capitalism Work* 159 (1996).

16. *Id.* at 167.

17. Melanie Kirkpatrick, "Rule of Law: Gay Marriage: Who Should Decide?" *Wall Street Journal* (March 13, 1996).

18. Richard Posner, *Sex and Reason* 313 (1992).

19. 478 U.S. 186 (1986).

20. See Griswold v. Connecticut, 381 U.S. 479 (1965) and its progeny.

21. Thomasson v. Perry, 80 F.3d 915 (4th Cir. 1996) (en banc).

22. Cf. Ben-Shalom v. Marsh, 881 F.2d 454 (7th Cir. 1989) (interpreting prior armed forces policy as not violating the First Amendment).

23. Re Layland and Minister of Consumer and Commercial Relations, 104 D.L.R. 4th 214 (Ontario Court 1993).

24. Re Attorney-General of Canada and Mossop, 100 D.L.R. 4th 658 (1993).

25. 124 D.L.R. 4th 609 (1995).

26. See generally Vogel v. Government of Manitoba, 126 D.L.R. 4th 72 (Manitoba Ct. Appeal 1995).

27. 132 D.L.R. 4th 538 (Ontario Court 1996).

28. 51 L.A.C. 4th 69 (Oct. 16, 1995).

29. See Re Carleton University and Canadian Union of Public Employees, Local 2424, 35 L.A.C. 3d 96 (June 10, 1988); Re Treasury Board (Indian & Northern Affairs) and Watson, 11 L.A.C. 4th 129 (April 30, 1990); Re Parkwood Hospital and McCormick Home, 24 L.A.C. 4th 149 (Jan. 17, 1992); Re Canada Post Corp. and Public Service Alliance of Canada, 34 L.A.C. 4th 104 (April 16, 1993); Re Freshwater Fish Marketing Corporation and United Steelworkers of America, Local 561, 49 L.A.C. 4th 139 (July 18, 1995).

30. 43 L.A.C. 4th 172 (Nov. 23, 1994).

31. 38 L.A.C. 4th 29 (Sept. 24, 1993).

32. See generally W v. G, 1996 NSW Lexis 2458 (Supreme Court of New South Wales, Feb. 2, 1996).

33. 852 P.2d 44 (Hawaii 1993).

34. 116 S.Ct. 1620 (1996).

35. Paul Barrett, "Court Rejects Ban on Laws Protecting Gays," *Wall Street Journal* (May 21, 1996) (quoting Suzanne B. Goldberg, a staff attorney with the Lambda Legal Defense Fund).

36. Plessy v. Ferguson, 163 U.S. 537, 559 (1896) (Harlan, J., dissenting) (as quoted in Romer v. Evans, 116 S.Ct. 1620, 1623 [1996]).

37. Editorial, "Rethinking Equality," *Wall Street Journal* (May 22, 1996).

38. 116 S.Ct. at 1630 (Scalia, J., dissenting).

39. Dillon v. Frank, 1992 U.S. App. LEXIS 766 (6th Cir. 1992).

40. Carreno v. IBEW Local No. 226, 54 FEP Cases 81 (D. Kan. 1990).

41. McCoy v. Johnson Controls World Services, 878 F. Supp. 229 (S.D. Ga. 1995).

42. Richard Epstein, *Forbidden Grounds* (1992).

43. 45 L.A.C. 4th 71 (Dec. 5, 1994).

44. See *New York Times*, national ed., C23 (Oct. 18, 1996) (excerpts from the second televised debate between Clinton and Dole, held on Oct. 16, 1996).

### Notes to Chapter 6

1. See Bigelow v. Bullard, 901 P.2d 630 (Nev. Supreme Ct. 1995).

2. See Ann C. McGinley, "Credulous Courts and the Tortured Trilogy: The Improper Use of Summary Judgment in Title VII and ADEA Cases," 34 *B.C. L. Rev.* 203 (1993). See also Ruth Colker, *Hybrid: Bisexuals, Multiracials and Other Misfits under American Law* (1996).

3. See Gilmer v. Johnson/Lane Interstate Corp., 500 U.S. 20 (1991).

4. See Symposium, "New York Stock Exchange, Inc., Symposium on Arbitration in the Securities Industry: Employment Discrimination," 63 *Fordham L. Rev.* 1613, 1613–14 (comments of Judith Vladeck) (1995).

5. See R. Blanpain and C. Engels, *International Encyclopedia for Labour Law and Industrial Relations*, ILO-11 (1994).

6. Visser v. Packer Eng'g Assocs., Inc., 924 F.2d 655, 657 & 660 (7th Cir. 1991) (en banc).

7. Barry Bluestone and Bennett Harrison, *The Deindustrialization*

*of America: Plant Closings, Community Abandonment, and the Dismantling of Basic Industry* 21 (1982).

8. See Melvin R. Solomon, "Between a Rock and a Hard Place: An Explanation of the Immigration Issues Facing Employers of Domestic Workers," 167 *N.J. Lawyer* 40 (Feb.-March 1995).

9. Facts on File, *World News Digest Facts on File* (Feb. 11, 1993).

10. William P. Quigley, "'A Fair Day's Pay for a Fair Day's Work': Time to Raise and Index the Minimum Wage," 27 *St. Mary's L.J.* 513, 531–32 (1996).

11. See Jennifer Middleton, "Contingent Workers in a Changing Economy: Endure, Adapt, or Organize?" 22 *N.Y.U. L. Rev. L. & Soc. Change* 557, 572 (1996).

12. See Solomon, *supra* note 8, at 40.

13. See Cornelius v. Sullivan, 936 F.2d 1143 (11th Cir. 1991).

14. See Wycklendt v. Weinberger, 381 F. Supp. 479, 483–84 (E.D. Wis. 1974) (grandmother who cared for four minor children denied retirement benefits).

15. See generally Reva B. Siegel, "Home as Work: The First Women's Rights Claims Concerning Wives' Household Labor, 1850–1880," 103 *Yale L.J.* 1073 (1994).

16. Christopher Jencks and Kathryn Edin, "The Real Welfare Problem," 1 *Am. Prospect* 31, 43–44 (1990).

17. Martha Albertson Fineman, "The Nature of Dependencies and Welfare 'Reform,'" 36 *Santa Clara L. Rev.* 287, 305 (1996).

18. *Id.* at 311.

19. See Ellis v. Chase Communications, Inc., 63 F.3d 473 (6th Cir. 1995).

20. See 29 C.F.R. §1975.6.

21. Middleton, *supra* note 11, at 558.

22. *Id.* at 567.

23. *Id.* at 570.

24. Chris Tilly, *Half a Job: Bad and Good Part-Time Jobs in a Changing Labor Market* 158 (1996).

25. *Id.* at 159.

26. *Id.* at 4.

27. *Id.* at 2 (citing economists who praise the part-time labor market as reflecting "innovation and flexibility" and "good for the U.S.").

28. Health Care & Retirement Corporation of America, 987 F.2d 1256 (6th Cir. 1993).

29. National Labor Relations Board v. Health Care & Retirement Corporation of America, 511 U.S. 571, 114 S.Ct. 1778 (1994).

30. Clyde W. Summers, "Worker Dislocation: Who Bears the Burden? A Comparative Study of Social Values in Five Countries," 70 *Notre Dame L. Rev.* 1033, 1067 (1995).

31. See Theodore J. St. Antoine, "The Model Employment Termination Act: A Threat to Management or a Long-Overdue Employee Right?" in Bruno Stein, ed., *Proceedings of New York University 45th Annual National Conference on Labor* 269, 270 (1993).

32. Carol Daugherty Rasnic, Balancing Respective Rights in the Employment Contract: Contrasting the U.S. 'Employment-at-Will' Rule with the Worker Statutory Protections against Dismissal in European Community Countries," 4 J. *Int'l L. & Prac.* 441, 444 (1995).

33. *Id.* at 463.

34. Summers, *supra* note 30, at 1043.

35. *Id.* at 1048–49.

36. First National Maintenance Corp. v. NLRB, 452 U.S. 666 (1981).

37. *Id.* at 690 (Brennan, J., and Marshall, J., dissenting).

38. 29 U.S.C. §2102.

39. See, e.g., Teamsters Local Union 413 v. Driver's Inc., 101 F.3d 1107 (6th Cir. 1996) (eleven different facilities in six states but not covered by federal plant-closing statute).

40. Rifkin v. McDonnell Douglas Corporation, 78 F.3d 1277 (8th Cir. 1996).

41. Loehrer v. McDonnell Douglas Corporation, 98 F.3d 1056 (8th Cir. 1996).

42. Bluestone and Harrison, *supra* note 7, at 4.

43. *Id.* at 182.

44. Summers, *supra* note 30, at 1044.

45. Bluestone and Harrison, *supra* note 7, at 241.

46. Tenn. Code Ann. §50–1–601(1).

# INDEX

# ABOUT THE AUTHOR

Ruth Colker is the Heck-Faust Memorial Chair in Constitutional Law at The Ohio State University College of Law and author, most recently, of *Hybrid: Bisexuals, Multiracials, and Other Misfits under American Law*.